Building Porches & Patios

COWLES
Creative Publishing, Inc.
Minnetonka, Minnesota, USA

Contents

Copyright © 1996
Cowles Creative Publishing, Inc.
Formerly Cy DeCosse Incorporated
5900 Green Oak Drive
Minnetonka, Minnesota 55343
1-800-328-3895
All rights reserved
Printed in U.S.A.

Books available in this series:
Everyday Home Repairs, Decorating With Paint & Wallcovering, Carpentry: Tools • Shelves • Walls • Doors, Building Decks, Kitchen Remodeling, Home Plumbing Projects & Repairs, Basic Wiring & Electrical Repairs, Workshop Tips & Techniques, Advanced Home Wiring, Carpentry: Remodeling, Landscape Design & Construction, Bathroom Remodeling, Built-in Projects for the Home, Kitchen & Bathroom Ideas, Refinishing & Finishing Wood, Exterior Home Repairs & Improvements, Home

Masonry Repairs & Projects, Building Porches & Patios, Deck & Landscape Ideas, Flooring Projects & Techniques, Advanced Deck Building

Library of Congress
Cataloging-in-Publication Data

Building porches & patios.

p. cm.--(Black & Decker home improvement library)
Includes index.
ISBN 0-86573-697-9 (hardcover).
ISBN 0-86573-698-7 (softcover).
1. Porches—Design and construction—Amateurs' manuals.
2. Patios—Design and construction—Amateurs' manuals. I. Cy DeCosse Incorporated. II. Series.
TH4970.B86 1996
690'.184--dc20   95-46568

![Cowles] COWLES
Creative Publishing, Inc.
Minnetonka, Minnesota, USA

President/COO: Nino Tarantino
Executive V.P./Editor-in-Chief:
 William B. Jones

Created by: The Editors of Cowles Creative Publishing, in cooperation with Black & Decker. **BLACK&DECKER** is a trademark of the Black & Decker Corporation and is used under license.

Group Executive Editor: Paul Currie
Project Manager: Ron Bygness
Editorial Director: Mark Johanson
Editor & Lead Researcher: Joel Schmarje
Editor & Technical Artist: Jon Simpson
Associate Creative Director: Tim Himsel
Art Directors: John Hermansen,
  Geoffrey Kinsey
Technical Production Editors: Dan Cary,
  Gary Sandin
Vice President of Development Planning &
  Production: Jim Bindas
Copy Editor: Janice Cauley
Contributing Editors: Ivy Chang, David
  Mahoney, Bryan Trandem
Shop Supervisor: Phil Juntti
Lead Set Builder: John Nadeau
Set Builders: Jon Hegge, Troy Johnson,
  Rob Johnstone

Production Staff: Helen Choralic, Deborah
  Eagle, Tom Hoops, Jeanette Moss,
  Michelle Peterson, Mike Schauer, Greg
  Wallace, Kay Wethern
Director of Photography: Mike Parker
Creative Photo Coordinator:
  Cathleen Shannon
Studio Manager: Marcia Chambers
Lead Photographer: Charles Nields
Photographers: Rex Irmen, Mike Parker,
  Greg Wallace
Contributing Photographers: Paul Najlis,
  Steve Smith
Contributing Photography: Archadeck;
  California Redwood Association; Lindal
  Cedar Homes Inc., Seattle, Wash.;
  Ned Skubic; Sticks and Stones Innovative
  Decks & Landscape Design; Wausau
  Tile, Inc., Wausau, Wis.
Production Manager: Jim Muñoz

Printed on American paper by:
  R. R. Donnelley & Sons Co.
00 99 98 97 / 5 4 3 2 1

Introduction

The porch and the patio are the traditional focal points for outdoor living. Few elements of your home will conjure up crisper images than the recollection of a breezy front porch on a perfect summer evening, or a holiday picnic with the family out on the patio. Investing in a new or updated porch or patio will create pleasant memories, and increase the value of your home.

This book features several of the most popular porch and patio projects, shown in step-by-step detail. Because the projects are presented as series of techniques, you can easily mix and match portions of each project to come up with a customized project that more closely meets your needs. For example, you can replace the combination storm windows shown in the patio enclosure project with screens and retaining strips installed using the same techniques shown in the porch screen-in project, creating a screened-in patio enclosure.

In *Building Porches & Patios,* you will find many useful do-it-yourself projects. Replace a plain front stoop with a traditional front porch; screen-in a porch so you can enjoy it even at the height of mosquito season; install a spacious paver or concrete patio in your backyard; add an arbor and trellis for a real touch of elegance; enclose a patio or porch with walls, windows and a roof.

Unlike other books that simply show a few basic techniques or give general plans, we take you step-by-step through actual porch and patio projects. Follow along as we give you an up-close look at the challenges encountered as we build a complete front porch from the ground up.

We also present a detailed look at a typical porch screen-in project. Whatever the size or shape of your porch, you can use the information in this project as a guide to improving your existing porch by adding screening. In the backyard, we show you how to design and lay out two major patio construction projects: a brick-paver patio that can be built without mortar or concrete, and a concrete patio with a decorative exposed-aggregate finish. If your existing patio does not

make your heart race when you look at it, we show you how to give it new life with a terra-cotta face-lift. Even if the old patio is in rough shape, you can install a new tile surface if you pour a simple concrete subbase, and we show you how to do that, too. Our book also includes fully illustrated projects showing you how to build a distinctive arbor and trellis over your patio. And, to wrap things up, we show a step-by-step patio enclosure project.

Building a porch or a patio is a major job that usually requires some help. We strongly recommend that you contact a professional designer or architect to help you plan a project that meets your needs and budget, while satisfying the requirements of your local building department. The information in this book will be a great help to you in making an efficient transition from plan to reality, but you must have a detailed, approved plan before you start.

NOTICE TO READERS

This book provides useful instructions, but we cannot anticipate all of your working conditions or the characteristics of your materials and tools. For safety, you should use caution, care, and good judgment when following the procedures described in this book. Consider your own skill level and the instructions and safety precautions associated with the various tools and materials shown. Neither the publisher nor Black & Decker® can assume responsibility for any damage to property or injury to persons as a result of misuse of the information provided.

The instructions in this book conform to "The Uniform Plumbing Code," "The National Electrical Code Reference Book," and "The Uniform Building Code" current at the time of its original publication. Consult your local Building Department for information on building permits, codes, and other laws as they apply to your project.

A screened-in patio or porch provides almost all the benefits of outdoor living, while providing protection from bad weather and pests. A screen-in can be accomplished around an existing structure, like a front porch (see pages 64 to 69), or under a second-story deck (see page 11). Or, you can build a whole new structure attached to or next to your home, complete with walls and a roof.

A Gallery of
Porch & Patio Ideas

Porches and patios come in many shapes and forms. Choosing the best design for your home is an important decision worthy of careful consideration. Seek out as much information as you can find—browse through magazines, walk through neighborhoods, visit libraries looking for ideas that you can incorporate into your porch or patio design. In most cases, borrowing elements from several designs can create a plan that is custom-fitted to meet your needs. Or, if you are lucky, you may even find the exact design that works for your project in one location.

The photographs on the following pages will give you an indication of the diversity of styles and designs that can be found in porches and patios. Use them as a starting point for gathering the ideas that eventually will become your new or updated porch or patio.

A basic front porch provides shelter at the front entry and gives a plain home a more distinguished, sophisticated appearance. A well-designed porch does not need to be fancy, but it should use the same basic design style and building materials used in the rest of the house.

Integrate different porch and patio elements by using similar design styles. The railing and the arbor above have unrelated functions, but they work well together in establishing a cohesive outdoor living area that creates good flow for traffic and for the eye.

Use sun filters or screening to increase your comfort outdoors. The filtering screen attached to the arbor above lessens the intensity of the sun and cuts down on wind. A trellis with climbing vines will have a similar effect, but it also creates a visual block, thereby increasing privacy or obstructing your view, depending on your perspective.

Consider decorating options when planning a porch or patio screen-in. Closing out the elements greatly expands your range of options when selecting furnishings. By selecting furnishings or decorating styles during the design process, you can also select window styles, wall coverings, and general building styles that complement your favorite decorating approach.

Choose your favorite elements, and combine them in ways that meet your needs (left). The look of a porch and the function of an arbor-and-trellis are effectively merged in the project shown.

Use existing structures, like a second-story walkout deck (right, top) as a framework for building a screened-in area. Provide insect blocking and rain protection (if desired) between the slats in any deck boards above the area (page 65).

Work with existing building materials and design style (right) to create a porch or patio that blends in and complements your home.

Consult a design professional to help you create a detailed construction plan for your project. Unless you have a great deal of experience with frame carpentry and house construction, you should have a professionally drawn plan before starting any major project, like adding a porch or a patio enclosure.

Planning a Porch or Patio Project

The adage "form follows function" applies as much to a porch or patio project as it does to any other structural design. Begin your planning by listing ways you would like to use your new porch or patio. Are you looking mainly for a comfortable spot where you can contemplate your garden in summer bloom, or do you want a light-filled place where you can enjoy your coffee and the morning paper throughout most of the year?

Next, take stock of your property. Is there room to build around your existing landscape elements without running afoul of local building and zoning restrictions? Is the proposed area exposed to direct sun or wind? Sketching a site drawing will help you assess these factors. Also consider the style and construction of your house. If you are thinking about adding a porch, for example,

would it look best with a peaked gable roof that matches your house roof, or would a flat shed roof blend in better? Once you have made some initial decisions about the project that is best for you, enlist the aid of an architect or a designer. He or she can help you develop ideas into detailed design drawings needed to obtain a building permit. Also consult your local building department. The inspectors there can supply you with information about building codes and other requirements that will affect your project.

This section shows:

Tips for Designing Your Project

Evaluate the planned project site: Note locations of windows, electrical service lines, and any other obstructions that might affect the positioning or design of a porch or a patio structure. For example, if you are interested in building a front porch, note the distance from the front door to any nearby windows— any design you come up with must be large enough

to include the window, or small enough to stop short of it. Also assess the building materials used in and around the planned project area. For example, the yellow stucco walls on the house at right would be a natural fit with any clay-based or earth-colored building materials, like terra-cotta patio tile.

Consider the roofline of your house for projects that are attached to the house and include their own roof. The house to the left had just enough second-floor exterior wall space that a porch could be attached to it without the need for tying the porch roof

directly to the roof of the house—a project for professionals only. The patio enclosure at the right takes advantage of the low, flat roof on the house expansion by extending the roofline to create the patio-enclosure roof.

(continued next page)

Measure your proposed project area, then draw a scale plan on which you can sketch ideas. Your plan should include relevant features such as shade patterns, trees, and other landscaping details. Also measure the height of door thresholds and the length and height of any walls or buildings adjacent to the proposed project area.

Measure the slope of the proposed building site to determine if you would need to do any grading work. Drive stakes at each end of the area, then tie a mason's string between the stakes. Use a line level to set the string to level. At each stake, measure from the string to the ground: the difference in the distances, when calculated over the distance between stakes, will give you the slope. If the slope is greater than 1" per foot, you may need to regrade the building site: consult a landscape architect.

Measure the roof slope of your house, and try to use the same slope if the project you are planning includes a roof. Hold a carpenter's square against the roofline with the long arm perfectly horizontal. Position the square so the long arm intersects the roof at the 12" mark. On the short arm, measure down to the point of intersection: the number of inches will give you the roof slope in a 12" span. For example, if the top of the square is 4" from the roofline, then your roof slope is 4-in-12.

Identify your siding type:

Stucco (above): If you have stucco siding, plan on a fair amount of work if your project requires you to remove siding—as when installing a ledger board. To remove stucco siding, first score the outline of the area to be removed with a chisel. Next, cut the stucco using a circular saw with a masonry blade. Make multiple passes, increasing the blade depth by ⅛" increments until the blade reaches the stucco lath. Chisel the stucco away inside the cut-out area, using a cold chisel, and cut out the lath with aviator snips.

Lap siding (below): Whether it is wood, aluminum, or vinyl, lap siding is much easier to remove than stucco, and it should not be considered an impediment when planning a project. To remove it, simply set the blade of a circular saw to a cutting depth equal to the siding thickness (usually about ¾") and make straight cuts at the edges of the removal area. Finish the cuts at the corners with a chisel, and remove the siding.

Learn about house construction. The model above shows the basic construction of a platform-framed house—by far the most common type of framing to-day. Pay special attention to locations of rim joists and framing members, since you likely will need to anchor any large porch or patio project to one or both of these elements.

Mark property lines and measure distances from the planned project area to municipal sidewalks or streets before developing a detailed project plan. To avoid future disputes, mark property lines as though they are 1 ft. closer in than they actually are.

Frost line

Concrete frost footings are required for many porch and patio projects—the frost line is the first point below ground level where freezing will not occur. Frost lines may be 48" or deeper in colder climates. Always build frost footings 1 ft. past the frost line.

Working with Inspectors & Building Codes

Any addition made to your house must comply with local zoning ordinances and building codes that specify where and how you can build.

In most areas, building codes are created by the building or planning department in your municipal government. These departments are staffed by inspectors, who are trained to answer questions, provide information, grant building permits, and make on-site inspections of some building projects. Get to know your local inspectors at the beginning of your project—view them as a helpful resource for a successful project.

The specific types of projects that require building permits varies between localities, but it is safe to say that any major project, like a new porch or a patio enclosure, will require a permit. To be granted a permit, you must present a detailed plan that includes both an elevation drawing and a floor plan (see photos, right). There are some very specific conventions you must follow in creating these drawings, so get assistance if you have not done this kind of work before. You also will be required to pay a permit fee, which likely is based on the projected cost of the project.

In some cases, projects that are designed to occupy space near property borders or municipal sidewalks or streets may require that you get a variance from your local zoning commission. Discuss this possibility with a local inspector.

Project Features Affected by Codes:

• **Construction materials:** Building codes often prescribe minimum sizes for structural members of your project, like deck joists, beams, posts, and ledgers.

• **Fasteners:** Screw sizes and spacing are usually indicated for most parts of the project, from structural elements to roof decking.

• **Total size:** Height, width, and estimated weight of the project must be suitable for the support methods used, and comply with any neighborhood covenants.

• **Footings:** Codes define what, if any, footing requirements affect your project (photo, left).

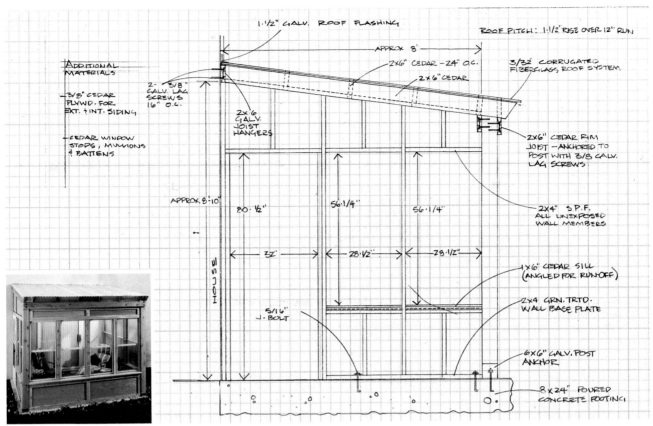

An elevation drawing shows sizes and locations of structural elements such as footing, ledger, studs, beams, rafters, door and window headers, as well as roof pitch and the type of roof covering planned. It also notes specific building materials and fasteners.

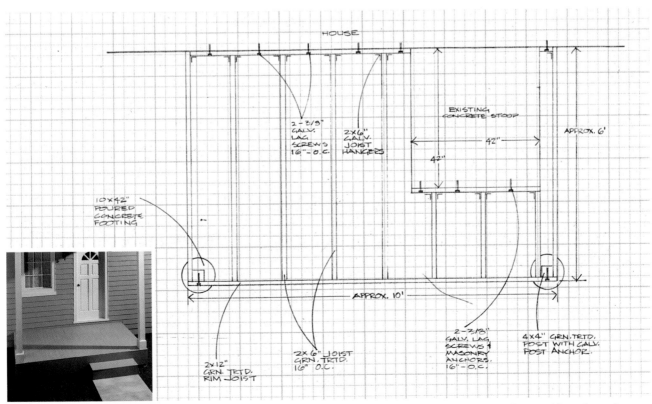

A floor plan shows overall project dimensions, the size and spacing of floor joists, the size and location of posts, and the types of hardware to be used for connecting and anchoring structural members.

Working Safely

Wear sensible clothing and protective equipment when working outdoors, including: a cap to protect against direct sunlight, eye protection when working with tools or chemicals, a particle mask when sanding, work gloves, full-length pants, and a long-sleeved shirt. A tool organizer turns a 5-gallon bucket into a safe and convenient container for transporting tools.

Working on porches or patios means working outdoors. By taking common-sense precautions you can work just as safely outdoors as indoors, even though the exterior of your house presents a few additional safety considerations.

Building projects for porches and patios frequently require that you use ladders or scaffolding. Learn and follow basic safety rules for working at heights.

Any time you are working outside, the weather conditions should play a key role in just about every aspect of how you conduct your work: from the clothes you wear to the amount of work you decide to undertake. Plan your work days to avoid working in extreme heat. If you must work on hot days, take frequent breaks and drink plenty of fluids.

Tips for Working Safely

• Work with a helper whenever you can. If you have to work alone, inform a friend or family member so he or she can check up on you periodically. If you own a portable phone, keep it handy at all times.

• Use cordless power tools when they will do the job—power cords are a frequent cause of worksite accidents. When using corded tools, plug them into a GFCI extension cord.

• Never work with tools if you have consumed alcohol or medication.

• Do not use power tools for tasks that require you to work overhead. Either find another way to access the task, or substitute hand tools.

Tips for Worksite Safety

Set up your worksite for quick disposal of waste materials. Use a wheelbarrow to transfer waste to a dumpster or trash can immediately. NOTE: Disposal of building materials is regulated in most areas—check with your local waste management department.

Create a storage surface for tools. Set a sheet of plywood on top of a pair of sawhorses to make a surface for keeping tools off the ground, where they are a safety hazard and are exposed to damage from moisture. A storage surface also makes it easy for you to locate a tool when needed.

Tips for Using Ladders

Do not stand on upper steps of stepladders, particularly when handling heavy loads.

Provide level, stable footing for extension ladders. Install sturdy blocking under ladder legs if the ground is uneven, soft, or slippery, and always drive a stake next to each ladder foot to keep the ladder from slipping away from the house.

Tools & Materials

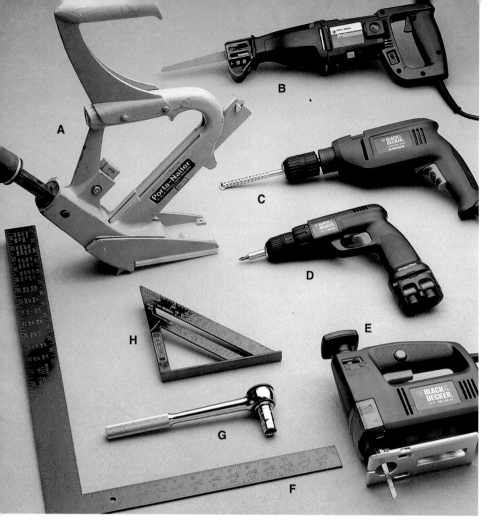

You probably already own many of the basic hand and power tools needed to complete the projects shown in this book. Others, such as a flooring nailer, you may have to rent. For almost every project in this book, start with a tool kit consisting of the basic tools listed below, and add specialty tools as needed.

Whenever you build outdoor projects, like porches and patios, use exterior-rated building materials and hardware whenever available. If you must use nonexterior-rated wood, like finish-grade pine, be sure to prime and paint it thoroughly.

Tools for porch construction include: flooring nailer (A), reciprocating saw (B), hammer drill with masonry bit (C), cordless drill (D), jig saw (E), carpenter's square (F), ratchet wrench (G), and speed square (H).

Basic Hand Tools:
- tape measure
- chalk line
- wood chisel
- circular saw
- pencil
- level
- hammer
- drill and bits

How to Use a Speed Square

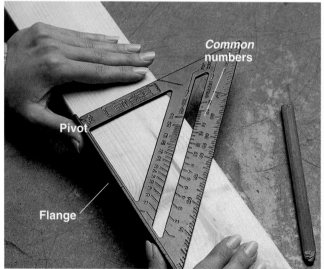

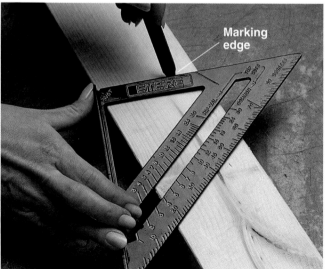

The speed square is a traditional roofer's tool that is very helpful for any projects that involve angle cutting. To use a speed square, you must either know or measure the slope of the line you want to mark, in inches per foot (page 14). Once you have the slope information, begin marking a cutting line onto a board by holding the flange of the speed square against the edge of the board. Look for the word *common* and the row of numbers aligned with it. Holding the end of the flange securely against the edge of the board, pivot the square so the *common* number equalling the rise of slope in inches per foot aligns with the same edge being pivoted against. Mark cutting line along the marking edge.

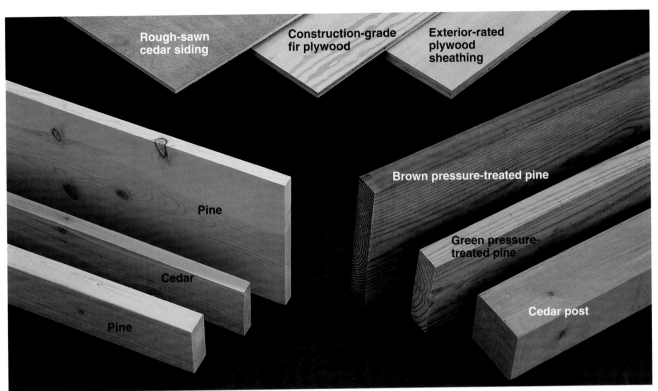

Lumber for porch and patio projects includes *sheet goods*, like ¼" cedar siding, ½" construction-grade plywood, and ¾" exterior-rated plywood sheathing. *Framing lumber* is usually 2x-dimensional lumber meant for strength, not appearance. It can be found in dimensions from 2 × 2 up to 2 × 12, and is available in cedar or green and brown pressure-treated pine. *Posts* can be cedar or treated pine. *Finish-grade lumber,* used for areas where appearance is important, is 1x-dimension pine or cedar.

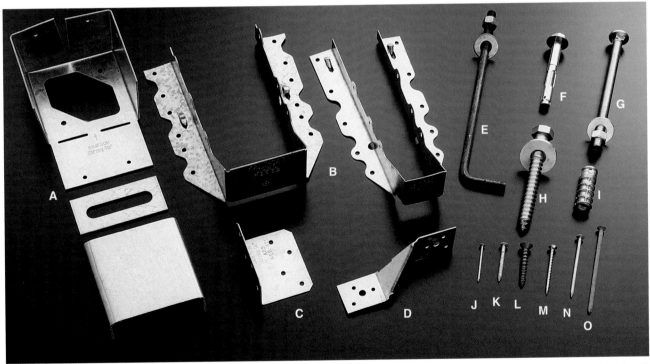

Connectors and fasteners include: post anchor with washer and pedestal (A), double- and single-joist hangers (B), angle bracket (C), rafter tie (D), J-bolt with nut and washer (E), masonry anchor bolt (F), carriage bolt with nut and washer (G), lag screw with washer (H), lead anchor sleeve (I), 4d galvanized nail (J), galvanized joist-hanger nail (K), self-tapping masonry screw (L), deck screw (M), 8d galvanized nail (N), and 16d galvanized nail (O).

Porch-building Projects

Add a new front porch to your home, or replace an old, worn structure with a brand-new porch. A simple porch like the one shown above blends in well with rustic or unadorned house styles. Or, you can add railings, steps, and other decorative features to match the style of your house.

Porch-building Projects

Whether it is located in the front, back, or side of your house, a porch is a prominent feature that should be built or updated only in accordance with a detailed plan. Working with a design professional, use your design ideas to create a plan for a new or updated porch that is attractive, functional, and within your budget.

The intent of the projects on the following pages is to demonstrate how to turn your building plan into a finished product. Do not attempt to create these projects without an approved plan of your own. In addition to a plan, you will need a building permit from your local building department for most porch projects.

The best porch designs reflect the style of the house, while meeting your needs for use. If you plan on spending many evenings relaxing on the porch, you will want a larger structure than if your main goal is provide shelter at the entry to your home. The same standards hold true for updating projects, like adding a railing to an open porch, or screening in a porch.

This sections shows:
• Building Porches (pages 26 to 53)
• Building & Installing Porch Railings (pages 54 to 57)
• Building Wood Porch Steps (pages 58 to 63)
• Screening in Porches (pages 64 to 69)

Options for Building & Updating Porches

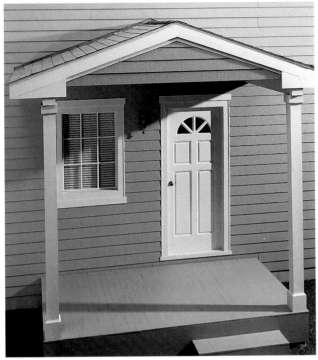

An open front porch is the simplest type of porch, but the deck can be no more than 20" above the ground in most areas. Because there are no railings, an open porch is a good choice for homeowners who like to visit with neighbors and passersby. Pages 26 to 53.

Porch railings are a necessary safety feature on porches that are 20" or more above the ground, but they are also an attractive design element that can be integrated into your new porch design, or added to your existing porch. Pages 54 to 57.

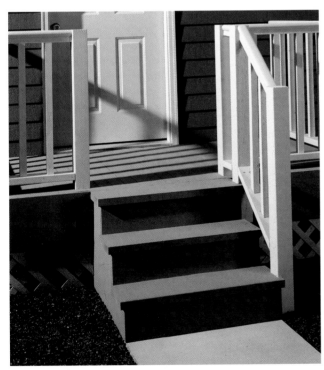

Wood porch steps are fairly easy to construct. Though not as maintenance-free as concrete steps, they better match the style of most porches. Step railings can be designed and built to match the porch railing. Pages 58 to 63.

Screened-in porches are very popular conversion projects for homeowners in areas where insects are a problem. The screening-in process is surprisingly simple. Pages 64 to 69.

After

Before

A front porch provides a sheltered entry point and creates a pleasant outdoor living space. Adding a new front porch gives your house a more sophisticated appearance.

Building Porches

Adding a front porch to your house is a major project. But with thorough preparation and a detailed construction plan, a successful porch-building project can be accomplished by most do-it-yourselfers.

A porch is a permanent part of your home, so make sure the foundation and structure are sturdy and meet all local building codes. Also pay close attention to design issues so the size and style of the porch make sense with the rest of your house. Use the techniques illustrated in this project as a guide to help you convert your own porch plan into a reality.

This project shows:

- How to Install Ledger Boards & Posts (pages 30 to 34)
- How to Install Deck Joists (pages 35 to 36)
- How to Install Porch Floors (pages 37 to 39)
- How to Install Beams & Trusses (pages 40 to 43)
- How to Install Roof Coverings (pages 44 to 46)
- How to Wrap Posts & Beams (pages 47 to 48)
- How to Finish the Cornice & Gable (pages 49 to 50)
- How to Install Soffits & Ceilings (pages 51 to 52)
- Tips for Applying Finishing Touches (page 53)

Anatomy of a Porch

The basic parts of a porch include the roof, the posts and beams, the floor and floor deck, the support system (ledger board and post footings), trim, and optional elements like railings and steps. See pages 28 to 29 for more information on these systems.

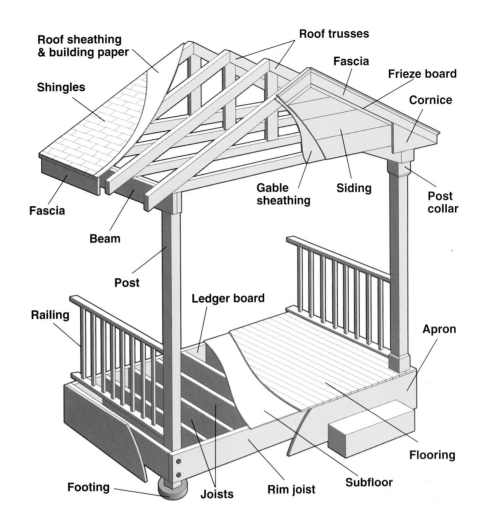

Roof sheathing & building paper

Roof trusses

Fascia

Frieze board

Shingles

Cornice

Gable sheathing

Siding

Post collar

Fascia

Beam

Post

Ledger board

Railing

Apron

Footing

Joists

Rim joist

Subfloor

Flooring

Tips for Building Front Porches

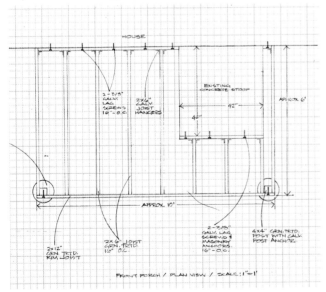

Rafter chords

Rafter tail

Bottom chord

Work from a construction plan. Because a porch is a permanent part of your house, you will need a building permit and a detailed construction plan before you start (pages 16 to 17). The plan should include a floor plan, like the one shown above, and an elevation drawing. For your convenience, also create a comprehensive materials list and an assembly plan.

Use pre-built roof trusses for porch construction. They are easier to work with than site-built rafters. When ordering trusses, you must know the roof pitch (page 14), the distance to be spanned, and the amount of overhang past the beams. Trusses can be purchased in stock sizes, or custom-ordered at most building centers—consult with the salesperson to make sure you get the right trusses for your project.

Elements of a Porch: The Foundation

Concrete footings, cast in tubular forms, support the porch posts. Post anchors, held in place with J-bolts, secure the posts to the footings. Frost footings, required for porches, should be deep enough to extend below the frost line, where they are immune to shifting caused by freezing and thawing.

Existing concrete steps with sturdy footings can be used to support the porch deck—an easier option than removing the concrete steps. Excavate around the steps to make sure there is a footing, and that it is in good condition.

Elements of a Porch: The Deck & Floor

Joist hanger

Ledger

Joist

Rim joist

A series of parallel joists supports the floor. Joist hangers anchor the joists to the ledger and the front rim joist, which acts like a beam to help support both the joists and the floor. Local building codes may contain specific requirements for thickness of the lumber used to make the rim joist. The face of the rim joist often is covered with finish-grade lumber, called an "apron," for a cleaner appearance.

Tongue-and-groove porch boards installed over a plywood subfloor is common porch-floor construction. The subfloor is attached to the joists. The porch boards, usually made of fir, are nailed to the subfloor with a floor nailer tool (page 20).

Elements of a Porch: The Posts & Beams

The posts and beams support the weight of the porch. Posts are secured by post anchors at the footings. Beams are connected to the posts with post saddles, and attached to a ledger board at the house using double-joist hangers. For most porch projects, doubled 2 × 6 or 2 × 8 can be used to build beams.

Wraps for posts and beams give the rough framing lumber a smoother, more finished appearance, and also make them look more substantial and in proportion with the rest of the porch. Use finish-grade 1 × 6 and 1 × 4 pine to wrap 4 × 4 posts.

Elements of a Porch: The Roof

The porch roof is supported and given its shape by sloped rafters or trusses. Prebuilt trusses, like those shown above, are increasingly popular among do-it-yourselfers. The ends of the trusses or rafters extend past the porch beams to create an overhang that often is treated with a soffit (pages 51 to 52). The trusses or rafters provide support and a nailing sur-

face for the roof sheathing, a layer of building paper, and the roofing materials—like asphalt shingles. The area of the porch below the peak of the roof, called the "gable," usually is covered with plywood sheathing and siding. Metal flashing is installed between the roof and the house to keep water out of the walls.

1 Lay out the location for the porch ledger board, based on your project plans. Mark the center of the project area onto the wall of your house to use as a reference point for establishing the layout. Measure out from the center and mark the endpoints of the ledger location. Make another mark ½" outside the endpoint to mark cutting lines for siding removal. According to most codes, the siding must be removed before the ledger board is installed.

2 Mark the ledger height at the centerline—if you are building over old steps, the top of the ledger should be even with the back edge of the steps. Use a straightedge and a level to extend the height mark out to the endpoints of the ledger location. Mark cutting lines for the ledger board cutout on the siding, ½" above the ledger location, then measure down from the top cutting line a distance equal to the width of the ledger board plus 1". Mark the bottom of the cutout area at that point, and extend the mark across the project area with the level and straightedge.

How to Install Ledger Boards & Posts

Ledger boards and posts support the roof and the deck of a porch. A ledger board is a sturdy piece of lumber, usually a 2 × 6 or 2 × 8, that is secured to the wall of a house to support joists or rafters for the porch. The posts used in most porch projects are 4 × 4 or 6 × 6 lumber that is attached to concrete footings with post-anchor hardware. Proper installation of the posts and ledgers is vital to the strength of the porch.

In most cases, porches are built with posts at the front only. A ledger is installed at deck level to support the floor, and another is sometimes installed at ceiling level to anchor the beams and the rafters or trusses.

If you are building your porch over an old set of concrete steps (page 28), make a cutout in the deck-level ledger board that is the same width and position as the steps, and attach the cut section to the top of the top step with masonry anchors.

Ledgers must be attached to the wall at framing member locations, or attached directly to the house rim joist (page 15) if the rim joist is at the correct height. Find and mark the framing member locations before starting ledger installation.

Everything You Need:

Tools: basic hand tools, caulk gun, framing square, mason's string, straightedge, plumb bob.

Materials: construction plans, framing lumber, drip edge flashing, caulk, concrete, tubular form, post anchor, joist-hanger nails, lag screws.

Drip-edge flashing

3 Remove the siding at the cutting lines (page 15). For wood siding, set the blade of a circular saw so it cuts to thickness of the siding, and cut along the cutting lines. Finish the cuts at the corners with a wood chisel. Remove the siding. You do not generally need to remove the wall sheathing between the siding and the framing members.

4 Cut a piece of metal or vinyl drip-edge flashing to fit the length of the cutout area. Apply caulk or exterior panel adhesive to the back face of the flashing—do not use fasteners to attach it. Slip the flashing behind the siding at the top of the cutout.

Ledger cutout

Rim joist

Deck joist location

Ledger

2 × 6 spacer

5 Cut a ledger board to the size specified in your construction plan. Because the end of the outer deck joist at each side of the project will butt against the wall sheathing in most cases, ledgers should be cut 4" shorter than the full planned width of the porch to create a 2" gap for the joist at each end. Also cut the rim joist for the porch (usually from 2 × 12 lumber) according to your project plans. Lay the ledger board next to the rim joist to gang-mark deck joist locations

onto the ledger and the rim joist. To allow for the difference in length between the ledger and the rim joist, set a 2 × 6 spacer at each end of the ledger. Mark the deck joist locations onto the ledger and the rim joist according to your construction plan. In the project above, we gang-marked deck joist locations 16" apart on center, starting 15¼" in from one end of the rim joist.

(continued next page)

Ledger-section location

Ledger-section location

OPTION: If you are attaching a section of the ledger to concrete steps (page 28), set the ledger in position on the back of the steps, and mark cutting lines onto the full-length ledger board at the edges of the steps. Cut at the cutting lines to divide the ledger into three sections.

6 Position the ledger board in the cutout area, up against the drip-edge flashing. Tack in place with duplex nails. Drill two counterbored pilot holes into the ledger at framing member locations, or at 16" intervals if attaching at the rim joist. Drive ⅜ × 4" lag screws, with washers, into the pilot holes to secure the ledger. Install all ledger sections that attach to the wall.

3 ft.

5 ft.

4 ft.

Front of project area

Mason's string

Project edge

Batter board

7 Establish square lines for the sides of the porch. First, build 3-piece 2 × 4 frames, called "batter boards," and drive one into the ground at each side, 12" past the front of the project area, aligned with the project edge. Drive a nail at each end of the ledger, and tie a mason's string to each nail. Tie the other

end of each string to a batter board. Square the string with the ledger, using the 3-4-5 method: mark the ledger board 3 ft. from the end, then mark the mason's string 4 ft. out from the same point. Adjust the mason's string until the endpoints from the 3-ft. and 4-ft. marks are exactly 5 ft. apart, then retie.

8 Mark locations for the centers of the porch posts onto the mason's strings by measuring out from the ledger board, using your construction plan as a guide. Use a piece of tape to mark the mason's string. Make sure the mason's string is taut.

9 Transfer the location for the post centers to the ground by hanging a plumb bob from the post marks on the mason's string. Drive a stake at the post-center location, then set an 8"-diameter tubular concrete form onto the ground, centered around the stake. Mark the edges of the form onto the ground, then remove the form and the stake, and dig a hole for the form past the frost-line depth (page 16). Avoid moving the mason's string. Set the tubular form into the hole so the top is about 2" above ground. Use a level to make sure the top of the form is horizontal. Excavate for and install both tubular forms.

(continued next page)

10 Fill the tubular forms with fresh concrete. Smooth the surface of the concrete with a trowel or float, then insert a J-bolt into the fresh concrete. Use a plumb bob to find the point on the surface of the concrete that is directly below the tape mark on each mason's string. Insert a J-bolt into the concrete at that point. The threaded end of the J-bolt should extend up at least 2". Let concrete cure for three days.

Post anchor

11 Set a metal post anchor over the J-bolt, and secure with a washer and nut. NOTE: Some post anchors have a pedestal that fits over the J-bolt to support the post (page 115). Cut a post that is at least 6" longer than the planned post height. With a helper, set the post into the post anchor and secure with 10d galvanized nails driven through the pilot holes in the post anchor. Install both posts.

12 Brace each post with a pair of 2 × 4s attached to stakes driven in line with the edges of the posts, but outside of the project area. Secure the posts to the stakes with deck screws, then use a level to make sure the posts are plumb. Attach the braces to the posts with deck screws.

Techniques for
Building Porches

How to Install
Deck Joists

With the support for the porch
project in place, begin installing
the deck joists. Joists usually
can be made from 2 × 6 lumber, but check your local codes
to be sure. Install them at the
edges of the project, and at 16"
intervals, perpendicular to the
house. Also install a 2 × 12
porch rim joist between the
front posts of the porch. For
drainage, the deck joists
should slope away from the
house at a rate of ⅛" per foot.

Everything You Need:

Tools: basic hand tools,
ratchet & socket set.

Materials: framing lumber, lag
screws, joist hangers, corner
brackets, masonry anchoring
hardware.

Level line

Slope line
(⅛" per foot)

1 With post braces still in place,
run a mason's string between a
post and the end of the ledger.
Use a line level to make sure the
string is level, then measure down
⅛" for every foot of distance between the ledger and the post to
establish a slope line. Mark a
slope line on each post.

2 Cut outer joists to fit between
the back of the ledger and the
front of each post, using the angle
created by the slope line and the
post as a guide for cutting the
ends of the joists. Attach the outer
joists to the ends of the ledger and
the posts with deck screws—you
may need to bend up the drip-
edge flashing above the ledger.

Ledger

Step ledger
(uninstalled)

3 Attach joist hangers to the ledger and to the rim
joist at the joist locations (step 5, page 31) with
galvanized joist-hanger nails. TIP: Slip a 2 × 6 scrap
into each hanger before nailing to make sure the
hanger holds its shape during installation.

4 Tack the porch rim joist in position: the top of the
rim joist should be flush with the tops of the outer
deck joists. Drill four counterbored pilot holes through
the rim joist and into each post, then drive ⅜ × 4" lag
screws with washers at each pilot hole to secure the
rim joist.

(continued next page)

5 Install metal corner brackets at each of the four inside corners, to stabilize the frame. Use joist-hanger nails to fasten the corner brackets.

6 Cut the remaining deck joists that fit all the way from the ledger to the porch rim joist—cut the same end angles that were cut for the outer joists (step 2, page 35). Install the deck joists in the joist hangers with joist-hanger nails.

Lag screw

Masonry sleeve

OPTION: If building over old steps, attach the step ledger board to the riser of the top step, using masonry anchors (inset). Lay a straightedge across the joists next to the steps as a reference for aligning the top of the ledger board. Shim under the ledger to hold it in position, then drill counterbored, ⅜"-diameter pilot holes for lag screws into the ledger. Mark the pilot

hole locations onto the riser, then remove the ledger. Drill holes for ⅜"-diameter masonry-anchor sleeves into the riser with a hammer drill and masonry bit. Drive the sleeves into the holes with a maul or hammer, then attach the step ledger with ⅜ × 4" lag screws driven into the masonry sleeves. Drive pairs of lag screws at 16" intervals.

Techniques for
Building Porches

How to Install
Porch Floors

Like most floors inside your house, a porch floor is made of a subfloor, usually plywood, topped with porch boards. The subfloor provides a stable base over the joists, which usually run parallel to the house for maximum strength. Porch boards are nailed directly to the subfloor—we rented a floor nailer for this task (page 20).

Everything You Need:

Tools: basic hand tools, caulk gun, speed square, jig saw, floor nailer, mallet, nail set, hand saw.

Materials: plywood, tongue-and-groove flooring, finish flooring, floor nailer nails, deck screws.

1 Begin laying the plywood subfloor—we used ¾"-thick exterior plywood. Measure and cut plywood so any seams fall over deck joists, keeping a slight (⅛") expansion gap between pieces. Fasten plywood pieces with 1½" deck screws. If installing the floor over old steps, apply exterior-grade construction adhesive to the steps to bond with the plywood.

Notch for post

Nailing cleat

2 Notch plywood to fit around posts. Also nail a 2 × 4 nailing cleat to the edges of the post that are not fitted against joists. Make sure the cleat is level with the tops of the joists.

3 Cut a starter board from a tongue-and-groove porch board by ripcutting the grooved edge off of the board with a circular saw. Cut the starter board 1" longer than finished length, including a ¾" overhang for the porch apron.

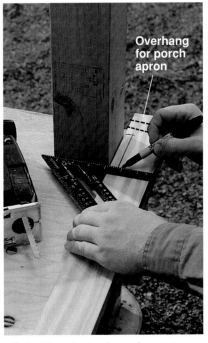

Overhang for porch apron

4 Set the starter board next to the post, with the tongue edge pressed against the post. Mark the location of the post onto the porch board, measure and mark the cutting depth to fit around the post, then notch the board with a jig saw.

(continued next page)

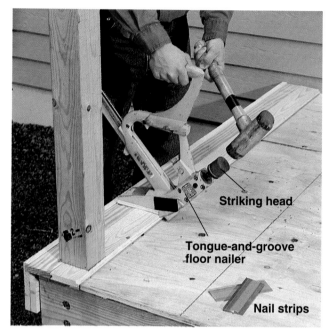

5 Make a cleat and spacer from scrap lumber the same thickness (usually ¾") as the skirt board you will install at the side of the porch. Sandwich the cleat and spacer together and attach them to the outer joist so the cleat is on the outside and at least 2" above the top of the joist. The spacer should be below the top of the joist. The cleat provides a secure, straight edge for aligning the first porch board, and the spacer creates an overhang for the skirt board.

6 Butt the notched porch board (step 4, previous page) against the cleat so it fits around the post, and nail in place. If using a tongue-and-groove floor nailer, load a nail strip, then position the nailer over the exposed tongue and rap the striking head with a mallet to discharge and set the nails. Nail at 6" to 8" intervals, then cut and position the next porch board (notched for the post, if needed) so the groove fits around the tongue of the first board, and nail in place.

7 Continue installing porch boards. Draw reference lines on the subfloor, perpendicular to the house, to check the alignment of the porch boards. Measure from a porch board to the nearest reference line occasionally, making sure the distance is equal at all points. Adjust the position of the next board, if needed.

8 Notch porch boards to fit around the other front post before you install them, then ripcut the last board to fit (create an overhang equal to the starter-board overhang). Position the last board, and drive galvanized finish nails through the face of the board and into the subfloor. Set the nail heads with a nail set.

¾" overhang

Front apron

9 Trim the exposed porch board ends so they are even. First, mark several porch boards ¾" out from the front edge of the rim joist to create an overhang that will cover the top of the apron (see next step). Snap a chalk line to connect the marks, creating a cutting line. Use a straightedge as a guide and trim off the boards at the cutting line with a circular saw. Use a hand saw to finish the cuts around the posts.

10 Cut aprons from exterior plywood to conceal the outer joists and the rim joist. Cut the side aprons (we used ¾"-thick plywood) so they fit flush with the front edges of the posts, then install them beneath the porch board overhangs and nail in place with 8d siding nails. After the side aprons are in place, cut the front apron long enough to cover the edge grain on the side aprons, and nail it to the rim joist.

OPTION: Build a wooden step and cover the surface with porch boards. The step above was built with a framework of 2 × 8s (toenailed to the front skirt), wrapped with exterior plywood, then covered with porch boards. See pages 58 to 63 for more information on building porch steps.

How to Install Beams & Trusses

Beams and trusses or rafters support the porch roof. Installing them takes patience and care. Use prebuilt trusses to simplify the project (page 29). Always have at least one helper on hand when you install trusses: they are awkward to handle. For beams, we used doubled 2 × 8s.

For information on installing the roof ledger, see pages 30 to 32.

Everything You Need:

Tools: basic hand tools, speed square, stud finder, torpedo level, hand saw, clamps, straightedge.

Materials: ladders, framing lumber, prebuilt roof trusses, double-joist hanger, nails.

1 Measure to find the midpoint of the porch deck and mark it on the house, then transfer the centerline to the peak area of the planned roof, using a straight 2 × 4 and a carpenter's level (page 119). Refer to your construction plan, then measure up from the porch deck and mark the top and bottom of the roof ledger onto the siding, near the center mark. Also mark the ledger height at the ends of the project area, then connect the height marks with a chalk line.

2 Mark a 2 × 6 to cut for the roof ledger by setting it on the deck so it extends past the edges of both front posts. Mark the outside edges of the posts onto the 2 × 6, then make another mark directly above each edge of the deck. Cut the ledger to length, and make a reference mark at the midpoint of the board.

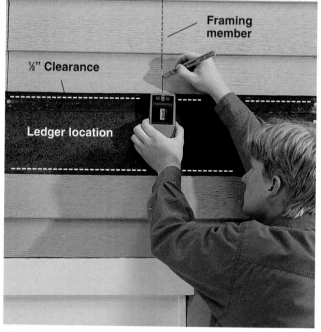

3 At the roof ledger outline on the wall, measure out in each direction from the centerpoint and finish the outline so it is the same length as the ledger board. Enlarge the outline by ½" on all sides, then remove the siding (page 15) in the outlined area. Use an electronic stud finder to locate framing members.

4 Attach the roof ledger with pairs of ⅜ × 4" lag screws driven at framing member locations (page 32). Lay out the locations for the beams onto the ledger, according to your construction plan. Insert a pair of 2 × 8 scraps into the double-joist hanger to help it keep its shape when you nail it. Position the hanger against the ledger, using a torpedo level to make sure it is plumb. Fasten the double-joist hangers to the ledger with joist-hanger nails.

5 Mark the front posts at the height of the bottoms of the double-joist hangers. To make sure the marks are level, set a straight board in each joist hanger and hold the free end against the post. Use a carpenter's level to adjust the height of the board until it is level, then mark the post where it meets the bottom of the straight board. Draw cutting lines on all sides of the post at the height mark.

6 Steady the post, and trim off the top at the cutting line. SAFETY TIP: Have a helper brace the post from below, but be careful not to drop the cutoff post end in the area.

7 Make the beams (we used pairs of 2 × 8s, cut to length, then nailed together with 16d common nails). The beams should extend from the double-joist hangers, past the fronts of the posts (1½" in our project). When nailing boards together to make beams, space nails in rows of three, every 12" to 16". For extra holding power, drive the nails at a slight angle.

(continued next page)

8 Lay out truss locations onto the tops of the beams, starting at the beam ends that will fit into the joist hangers. Mark both edges of each truss, drawing an "X" between the lines for reference. Generally, trusses should be spaced at 24" intervals—check your construction plan for exact placement.

9 Set a metal post saddle onto the top of each front post, and nail in place with joist-hanger nails. With a helper, raise the beams and set them into the post saddles and double-joist hangers. Secure the beams in the double-joist hangers with joist-hanger nails.

Spacer

10 If your beams are thinner than your posts (as above) cut plywood spacers and install them between the inside edges of the beams and the inner flange of the post saddle. The spacers should fit snugly, and be trimmed to roughly the size of the saddle flanges. Drive joist-hanger nails through the caps, into the spacers and beams.

Project centerline

11 With help, hoist the first truss into position. Turn trusses upside down to make them easier to handle when raising. Rest one end of the truss on a beam, then slide the other end up and onto the opposite beam. Invert the truss so the peak points upward, and position it against the house, with the peak aligned on the project centerline.

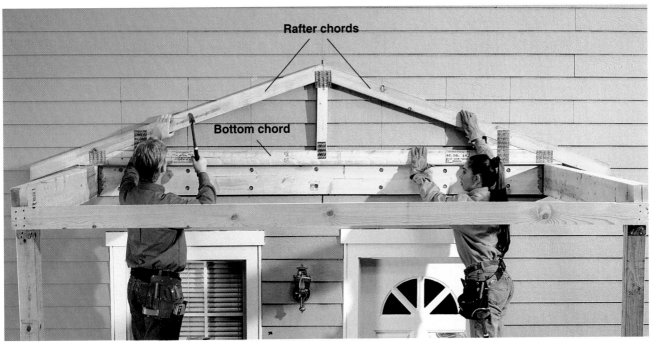

Rafter chords

Bottom chord

12 Make sure the first truss is flush against the siding, with the peak aligned on the project centerline. Nail the rafter chords and bottom chord of the truss to the house at framing member locations, using 20d common nails. Lift the remaining trusses onto the beams. TIP: If you are installing trusses with a pitch of 4-in-12 or less, you may find it easier to lift all trusses onto the beams before continuing with installation. For steeper pitches, lift and nail trusses one at a time.

13 Install the rest of the trusses at the locations marked on the beams, working away from the house, by toenailing through the bottom chords and into the beams with 8d nails. Nail the last truss flush with the ends of the beams. NOTE: If the bottom chord of the first truss overhangs the beams, install the rest of the trusses with equal overhangs.

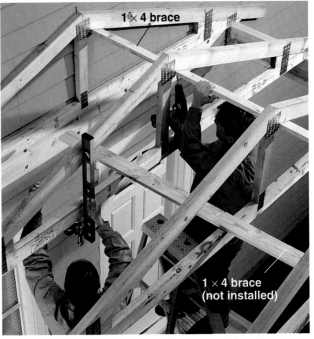

1 × 4 brace

1 × 4 brace (not installed)

14 Attach 1 × 4 braces to the underside of each row of rafter chords. Use a level to plumb each truss before fastening it to the braces with 2" deck screws.

Nailing strip

Techniques for Building Porches

How to Install Roof Coverings

The roof covering for a porch includes plywood roof sheathing, building paper, shingles, fascia boards, and other trim pieces. If you have never installed roof coverings before, get additional information on roofing techniques.

Everything You Need:

Tools: basic hand tools, ladder, hand saw, reciprocating saw, aviator snips.

Materials: plywood sheathing, finish-grade lumber, 30# building paper, metal roll flashing, 3-tab shingles, roofing nails, drip-edge flashing, roof cement.

1 Cut and attach 2 × 4 nailing strips to the rafter chords of the front truss, using 2½" deck screws. Nailing strips create a nailing surface for the roof sheathing overhang. Cut them to the same dimensions as the rafter chords.

Rafter tail

2 Cut ¾" exterior-grade plywood sheathing to cover the trusses and nailing strips. The sheathing should be flush with the ends of the rafter tails. Cut sheathing pieces so seams fall over rafter locations, and install them with 8d siding nails or deck screws.

3 Fill in the rest of the sheathing, saving the pieces that butt together at the peak for last. Leave a ¼" gap at the peak.

44

4 Cut ½"-thick plywood to cover the gable end of the roof. Measure the triangular shape of the gable end, from the bottom of the truss to the bottoms of the nailing strips. Divide the area into two equal-sized triangular areas, and cut plywood to fit. Butt the pieces together directly under the peak, and attach them to the front truss with 1½" deck screws.

5 Cut 1 × 4 frieze boards to fit against the plywood gable sheathing, beneath the nailing strips. Attach the frieze boards to the gable sheathing with 1¼" deck screws. Then, cut fascia boards long enough to extend several inches past the ends of the rafter tails. Nail the fascia boards to the nailing strips, with the tops flush with the tops of the roof sheathing.

6 Measure for side fascia boards that fit between the house and the back faces of the gable-end fascia boards. Cut the fascia boards to fit, then attach with galvanized 8d finish nails driven into the ends of the rafter tails. Make sure the tops of the fascia boards do not protrude above the plane of the roof sheathing. NOTE: If you plan to install soffits, use fascia boards with a plowed groove for soffit panels.

7 Trim off the ends of the gable-end fascia boards so they are flush with the side fascia boards, using a handsaw. Drive two or three 8d finish nails through the gable-end fascia boards and into the ends of the side fascia boards.

(continued next page)

Circular-saw cut

Step flashing

8 Remove siding above the roof sheathing to create a recess for metal roof flashing. Make a cut about 2" above the sheathing, using a circular saw with the cutting depth set to the siding thickness. Then make a cut flush with the top of the roof, using a reciprocating saw held at a very low angle. Connect the cuts at the ends with a wood chisel and remove the siding. See page 15 for more information on removing siding.

9 Install building paper, drip-edge flashing, and shingles as you would for a standard roofing project (see *Exterior Home Repairs,* Black & Decker Home Improvement Library). Slip pieces of metal step flashing behind the siding above the cutout area as you finish rows of shingles, sealing the seams with roof cement.

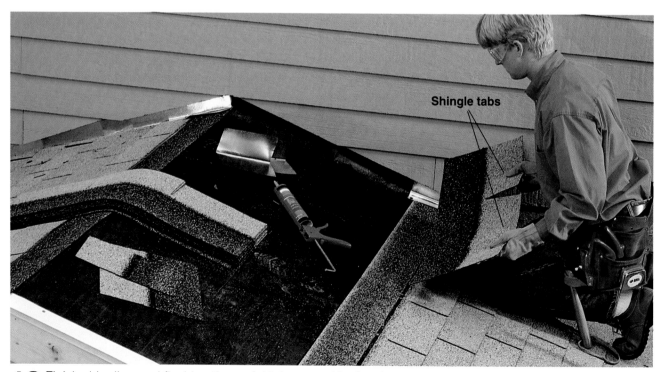

Shingle tabs

10 Finish shingling and flashing the roof. Make sure shingle tabs are staggered in regular patterns, with a consistent exposed area on shingle tabs. Cut off shingle tabs and use them to create the roof ridge.

How to Wrap
Posts & Beams

Even in the simplest front porch, standard posts and beams can look spindly and plain. Rather than spending the money for large timbers, it is a common practice among builders to wrap the posts and beams with finish-grade lumber to give them a more proportional look. We used finish-grade pine to give the posts in our porch project the appearance of solid 6 × 6 stock, and to conceal the fact that our beams are actually made from doubled 2 × 8s.

Everything You Need:

Tools: basic hand tools.

Materials: finish lumber, siding nails, plywood strips.

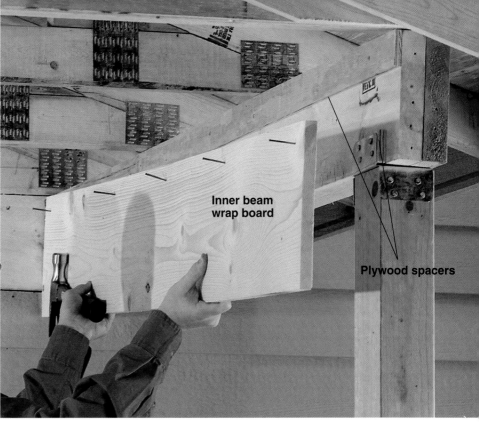

Inner beam wrap board

Plywood spacers

1 Cut wrap boards for the inner sides of the beams to the same length as the beams, using finish lumber wide enough to cover the beams and any metal saddles or joiners. We used 1 × 10, but sanded ¾" plywood can be used instead. Attach the inner side boards to the beams with 8d siding nails—in the project above, we added ½" plywood strips at the top and bottom of the beam to compensate for the ½" spacers in the metal post saddles.

Side board

Bottom board

2 Cut strips of wood to cover the bottoms of the beams. Position each strip next to a board cut the same size as the inner beam wrap. The difference in length between the side board and the bottom board should equal the distance of the beam overhang at the post. Preassemble the bottom board and side board by driving 8d finish nails at the butt joint, making sure to keep the joint square. Attach the assembly to the beam so the free end of the bottom board forms a butt joint with the inner beam wrap board.

3 Cut boards to create an end cap for each beam— we cut a piece of 1 × 10 to fit over the ends of the beam and the beam wrap, and attached it to a piece of 1 × 4 cut to cover the gap beneath the beam overhang. Nail end caps over the end of each beam.

(continued next page)

4 Cut boards for wrapping the posts so they span from the floor to the bottoms of the wrapped beams. For a 4 × 4 post, two 1 × 4s and two 1 × 6s per post can be used. Nail a 1 × 6 to the front of the post, overhanging ¾" on the outside edge. Nail a 1 × 4 to the outer face of the post, butted against the 1 × 6.

5 Preassemble the other two wrap boards, nailing through the face of the 1 × 6 and into the edge of the 1 × 4. Set the assembly around the post, nailing the 1 × 6 to the post and nailing through the other 1 × 6 and into the edge of the 1 × 4 (there will be a slight gap between the second 1 × 4 and the post).

6 Cut pieces of finish lumber to fit around the bases of the posts (called "post collars"). We used 1 × 6 to create the bottom post collars, and 1 × 4 to create the top collars where the posts meet the beams. Nail the collars together with 4d finish nails. TIP: Cut pieces so the front collar board covers the end grain of the side boards.

Furring strip

7 Roof ledgers often are visible after the porch ceiling is installed, so cover the ledger with finish lumber. If the ledger protrudes past the siding, cut a furring strip to cover the gap between the inside face of the ledger cover and the siding. Cut the ledger cover and furring strips to fit, and install with 8d nails. If the ledger extends past the outer face of the beam, the easiest solution is to paint it to match the siding.

Techniques for
Building Porches

How to Finish
the Cornice & Gable

The gable and the cornice are prominent features on the front of any porch. The gable is the area just below the peak, which is usually covered with trim and siding material. TIP: Paint siding materials before installation. The cornice, sometimes called the "cornice return" or the "fascia return," is usually fitted with trim that squares off the corner where it meets the soffit.

Everything You Need:

Tools: basic hand tools, miter box, straightedge guide.

Materials: plywood, framing lumber, finish-grade lumber, cove molding, nails, caulk.

Gable trim

Cornice

The cornice and gable are finished to match the siding and trim on your house. Use plywood or finish-grade lumber to make the cornice, and use siding that matches your house for the gable trim. Caulk seams at the peak of the gable, and between the fascia boards and the cornice (inset).

How to Install a Cornice

1 At each end of the front porch, measure the area from the end of the gable fascia to a spot about 6" inside the porch beam. Lay out a triangular piece of plywood or finish-grade lumber to fit the area, using a carpenter's square to create right angles. Cut out the cornice pieces, using a circular saw and straightedge.

2 Test-fit the cornice pieces over the ends of the porch gable, then install with 8d finish nails driven into the ends of the beams, and 4d nails driven up through the ends of the cornice pieces and into the underside of the gable fascia. Use a nail set to embed the heads of the nails below the surface of the wood, being careful not to split the cornice pieces.

How to Install Gable Trim

Gable fascia

Frieze board

1 Measure the dimensions of the area covered by the gable sheathing (page 45) on the house. If you have installed fascia and frieze boards, measure from the bottom of the frieze boards. Add 2" of depth to the area to make sure that siding will cover the edge of the ceiling once the ceiling and soffits are installed (pages 51 to 52). Snap a horizontal chalk line near the bottom of the gable sheathing to use as a reference line for installing the siding.

2 Mark a cutting line that matches the slope of the roof onto the end of one piece of siding. Use a framing square or a speed square (page 20) to mark the slope line. OPTION: Position a scrap board on the horizontal chalk line on the gable sheathing, and mark the points where the edges of the board intersect with the frieze board: connect the points to establish the slope line. Cut the siding or scrap board on the slope line and use it as a template to mark siding for cutting. Cut the bottom siding board to length.

3 Use 4d siding nails to install the bottom siding board so it is flush with the bottom edges of the frieze boards—the bottom edge of the siding board should be 2" lower than the bottom of the gable sheathing. Cut the next siding board so it overlaps the first board from above, creating the same amount of exposed siding as in the rest of the house. Be careful to keep the siding level. Continue cutting and installing siding pieces until you reach the peak of the gable.

Techniques for Building Porches

How to Install Soffits & Ceilings

Soffits are panels that close off the area between rafter ends and the side of the porch. They can be nailed directly to the rafters, or attached to nailers on the porch beams so they are horizontal. A porch ceiling can be made from plywood or tongue-and-groove boards to give the porch a finished appearance.

Everything You Need:

Tools: basic hand tools, straightedge guide, torpedo level, caulk gun, miter box.

Materials: plywood, plowed fascia board, nails, nailer.

Plowed groove

Option: Attach soffit directly to rafters. Attach a fascia board with a plowed groove (inset) to the rafter ends (page 45, step 6). Measure from the back of the fascia plow groove to the beam, following the bottom of the rafter tail, to establish the required width for the soffit panel. Measure the length from the house to the cornice or gable, then cut a piece of ⅜"-thick plywood to these dimensions. Insert one edge of the plywood panel into the plowed groove, and press the soffit panel up against the rafter tail. Nail the panel in place with 4d galvanized common nails, then caulk the edges before painting the panel.

How to Install Horizontal Soffit Panels

1 Install a fascia board with a plowed groove (page 45, step 6). Use a torpedo level to transfer the top height of the groove to the beam, near one end. Mark the groove height at the other end of the beam, then connect with a chalk line. Install a 2 × 2 nailer just above the chalk line.

2 Measure from the back of the plowed groove to the beam, just below the nailer, to find the required width of the soffit panel. Measure the length, then cut a piece of ⅜"-thick plywood to fit. Insert one edge of the soffit panel into the plow, then nail the other edge to the nailer with 4d nails.

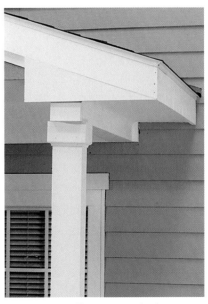

TIP: Paint soffits to match the rest of the porch trim. Add quarter-round molding at the joint between the soffit and the beam, or fill the gaps with tinted exterior-grade caulk.

How to Install a Porch Ceiling

1 To create nailing surfaces for ceiling materials, cut 2 × 4s to fit between rafters, spaced 24" on center, and flush with the bottoms of the rafters. NOTE: If you plan to install ceiling lights, have them wired before proceeding.

2 Measure the ceiling space and cut ceiling materials to fit (we used 4 × 8 sheets of ⅜"-thick plywood). Cut ceiling pieces so the seams fall on the centers of the rafters and nailing strips. Use 4d galvanized nails to attach the plywood to the rafters and nailers. Space nails at 8" to 12" intervals. Do not drive nails next to one another on opposite sides of joints.

3 Install molding around the edges of the ceiling to cover the gaps and create a more decorative look. Simple ¾" cove molding, which does not require any complicated coping cuts or installation techniques, is used for the above project. Miter the corners and attach with 4d finish nails. Set the nail heads slightly, then cover with wood putty before painting.

Techniques for
Building Porches

Tips for Applying Finishing Touches

A few final touches add per-
sonality and a completed look
to your porch-building project.
There are a wide range of decorative trim types that can be
purchased or built, then installed to dress up the porch or
help it blend with the style of
your house. Look through millwork catalogs to find ideas for
trimming out your new porch.
Also visit salvage yards to find
authentic millwork, like ginger-
bread types, that will blend in
with the rest of your house.

Avoid getting carried away with
decorative trim. A few elegant
touches will go a long way.

Use gable ornamentation to soften the hard lines of the gable peak.
Fan-style trim (above) and many other trim types that fit into a peak are
made to fit a range of different peak angles. Make sure to measure your
peak angle carefully before purchasing or ordering gable ornamentation.

Install decorative trim to enhance the appeal of
your porch. The scalloped fascia boards above were
cut from plain 1 × 6 pine, using a jig saw, to add a
touch of flair to a plain porch gable.

Put stock moldings, sold at any building center, to
creative use on a porch. The simple cove molding
above is installed at the joint between a post collar
and the post, to create more graceful lines.

Add preformed post caps to posts that support porch railings. Post caps are sold in a wide range of styles and sizes at most building centers. Most are attached by driving finish nails through the top of the cap and into the post. Others (photo below) are screwed into the post top with preinstalled screws.

Building & Installing Porch Railings

A porch railing not only provides security from falls, but can also make an important contribution to the visual appeal of a porch. The basic components of a railing are the railing posts, the bottom and top rails, the balusters, and optional cap rails. It is usually easiest to assemble the railing before you install it. Check local codes before designing a railing. In most cases, railings should be at least 36" high, and the spaces between balusters and between the porch floor and bottom rail should be no more than 4".

Everything You Need:

Tools: basic hand tools, speed square, ratchet and socket set.

Materials: plywood, framing lumber, post caps, milled rail caps, lag screws, screws, siding rails.

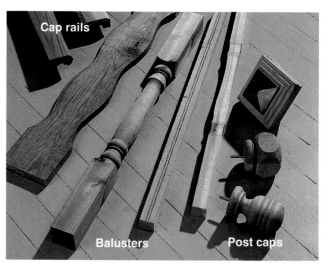

Railing components include decorative cap rails that are grooved to fit over a 2 × 2 railing; balusters, sometimes called spindles, that range from plain 2 × 2s to ornate millwork; and decorative post caps.

How to Build & Install a Porch Railing

1 Make a base plate for the railing post from two pieces of ¾"-thick plywood. Cut the plywood pieces to match the finished size of the post, including any post wrap boards (page 48). Stack the pieces together and fasten with 1¼" screws and construction adhesive. Do not put screws in corners.

2 Cut the post to finished height (usually 38" to 40"), allowing for the thickness of the base plate. If you plan to wrap the post, use scrap lumber the same thickness as the wrap boards to center the post on the base plate. Attach the base plate to the bottom of the post with three counterbored ⅜" × 4" lag screws.

3 Set the post in position on the porch floor. Drive ⅜" × 4" lag screws through pilot holes at each corner of the base plate, and into the porch floor.

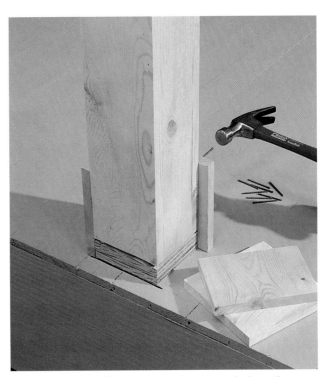

4 Cut and install wrap boards to match the other porch posts (page 48). Also cut and install collar boards to cover the edges of the base plate and the bottom of the post.

(continued next page)

5 Cut the top, bottom, and cap rails to length, using a circular saw. The bottom rail will have to be cut shorter than top and cap rails if you have installed collars at the post base. For our railings, we used 2 × 4s for the bottom rails, 2 × 2s for the top rails, and milled cap rails installed over the top rails.

6 Mark baluster layout onto the top and bottom rails—make sure balusters will be no more than 4" apart when installed. Drill ⅛"-diameter pilot holes all the way through the rails at the baluster layout mark, centering the holes from side to side.

7 If cutting your own balusters, clamp, measure, and cut the balusters to finished length. To save time and ensure uniform length, gang-cut the balusters, using a circular saw.

Spacing block

Shims

8 Lay the top and bottom rails on a worksurface. Use shims to support the balusters and top rail so they align with the center of the bottom rail. Attach the balusters to the rails by driving 2½" deck screws through the pilot holes in the rails, and into the baluster ends. TIP: Use a spacing block to keep balusters from shifting when they are attached.

9 Insert railing assembly between posts, using blocks to support it at the desired height. Drill ⅛" angled holes through the ends of the top and bottom rails and into the posts. Toenail railings to posts with 8d casing nails.

10 Slip the cap rail over the top rail. Attach the cap rail by driving 2½" deck screws at 18" intervals, up through the top rail and into the cap rail.

Variation: How to Install a Porch Rail Between Round Posts

1 Assemble railings and balusters (page 56). Position the assembly between the posts. Mark the top and bottom of each rail onto the posts. Cut along the lines with a handsaw, then use a chisel to remove wood between the cuts.

2 Install the railing assembly by inserting the rail ends into the post notches. Toenail the rail ends to the posts.

3 Set a compass to the post radius, then scribe an arc on each end of a cap rail. The distance between the arcs should equal the distance between posts. Cut out the arcs with a jig saw. Attach cap rail to top rail (step 10, above).

Wooden porch steps are easier to build and less expensive than concrete steps. With paint and the appropriate railing design, they can also be made to match the look of the porch.

Building Wood Porch Steps

Wood porch steps consist of three basic parts. Stringers, usually made from 2 × 12s, provide the framework and support for the steps. Treads, made from 2 × 12s or pairs of 2 × 6s, are the stepping surfaces. Risers, usually made from 2 × 8s, are the vertical boards at the back of each step.

If you are replacing steps, use the dimensions of the old steps as a guide. If not, you will need to create a plan for the new steps, which takes a little bit of math and a little bit of trial and error (see next page).

In addition to the step dimensions, consider style issues when designing steps, and if there are two or more steps, include a step railing that matches your existing porch railing.

Porch steps should be at least 3 ft. wide—try to match the width of the sidewalk at the base of the step area. To inhibit warping and provide better support, use three stringers, not two. Wood steps do not require footings. Simply attach them to the rim joist or apron of the porch, and anchor them to the sidewalk at the base of the first step.

Everything You Need:

Tools: basic hand tools, framing square, hand saw, wrench.

Materials: framing lumber, finish lumber, milled cap rail, corner brackets, carriage bolts, self-tapping concrete screws, deck screws.

Tips for Building Steps

Remove the old steps, if any, from the project area. With the old steps removed, you can better evaluate the structure of the porch to make a plan for anchoring the new steps. If possible, attach the step stringers directly to the porch rim joist or to the apron. Also evaluate the condition of the sidewalk to make sure it is strong enough to support the steps.

Make a detailed plan for the steps, keeping in mind that each step should be 10" to 12" deep, with riser height between 6" and 8". Make sure the planned steps conform to the required overall rise and run (photos, below).

How to Measure Rise & Run

1 Attach a mason's string to the porch floor. Drive a stake where you want the base of the bottom step to fall. Attach the other end of the string to the stake, and use a line level to level it. Measure the length of the string—this distance is the overall run of the steps.

2 Measure down from the string to the bottom of the stake to determine the overall height, or *rise*, of the steps. Divide the overall rise by the estimated number of steps. The rise of each step should be between 6" and 8". For example, if the overall rise is 21" and you plan to build three steps, the rise of each step would be 7". It is very important that all risers and all treads are uniform in size.

How to Build Porch Steps

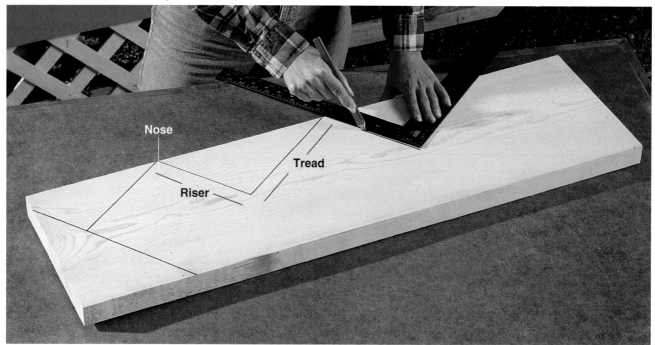

1 Mark the step layout (page 59) onto a board—usually a 2 × 12—to make the step stringers. Use a carpenter's square with the rise distance and run distance each noted on a leg of the square. Lay out the stringer so the "nose" areas where the tread and riser meet on each step fall at the same edge of the board. Check all angles with the square to make sure they are right angles.

2 Cut out the stringer, using a circular saw for straight cuts, and finishing the cuts with a handsaw where cuts meet at inside corners. Use this stringer as a template for laying out and cutting two more stringers. Mark and trim off the thickness of one tread (1½") at the bottom of each stringer so the rise of the bottom step will equal the rise of the other steps.

3 Attach evenly spaced metal angle brackets to the porch rim joist or apron, making sure the brackets are perpendicular to the ground. Position the stringers inside the angle brackets so the top of each stringer is 1½" below the top of the porch floor. Attach the stringers to the angle brackets with joist-hanger nails.

4 Measure the distances between the stringer tops, then use these measurements to cut two 2 × 4 cleats to length. Making sure stringers are square to the rim joist, attach the cleats to the concrete between the bases of the stringers, using self-tapping concrete screws driven into pilot holes.

5 Cut posts for the step railing to height, and attach them to the outside face of an outer stringer using 6" carriage bolts. Use a level to set the posts so they are plumb, then clamp them in position while you drill guide holes for the carriage bolts through the posts and the stringer. Drive the carriage bolts through the guide holes and secure each with a washer and nut on the inside face of the stringer.

6 Cut the risers and treads to length, using a circular saw. TIP: A 1" to 2" overhang at each outer stringer creates more attractive steps. Notch the treads for the top and bottom steps to fit around the posts, using a jig saw. Attach the risers to the vertical edges of the stringers, using 2½" deck screws, then attach the treads.

(continued next page)

7 Mark a 2 × 4 to use for the lower railing (see pages 54 to 57 for information on building railings). To mark the 2 × 4 for cutting, lay it on the steps flush against the posts, then mark a cutting line on the 2 × 4 at each inside post edge. Use the 2 × 4 as a template for marking cutting lines on the top and cap rails.

8 Set the blade of a circular saw to match the angle of the cutting marks on the 2 × 4, and gang the 2 × 4 with a 2 × 2 for the top railing and a piece of cap rail for cutting. Gang-cut the rails at the cutting lines.

9 Attach the bottom rail to the posts with deck screws driven toenail style through pilot holes and into the inside faces of the posts. The bottom of the rail should be level with the noses of the steps. Attach the 2 × 2 top rail so it is parallel to the bottom rail, 2" down from the finished post height.

10 Hold a 2 × 2 flush against a post so the ends extend past the top and bottom rails. Mark cutting lines on the 2 × 2 at the bottom edge of the top rail, and the top edge of the bottom rail. Use the 2 × 2 as a template for marking cutting lines on all railing balusters.

11 Mark layout lines for the balusters on the top and bottom rails, spacing the balusters no more than 4" apart. Drill ⅛" holes in the center of the top rail at baluster locations, then drive 2½" deck screws into the baluster ends. Toenail balusters to the bottom rail with 8d finish nails. Attach the cap rail (page 57).

12 Install a bottom rail, top rail, and cap rail in a horizontal position between the railing post at the top step and the end post for the porch railing. If the distance between posts is more than 4", install balusters between the rails.

13 Close off any open areas under the stringers with wood or lattice panels. First, attach nailing strips to the undersides of the outer stringer, set back far enough to create a recess for the wood or lattice. Cut a piece of wood or lattice to fit, and install. Attach decorative post caps (page 54) if desired, but first double-check the step post tops with a straightedge to make sure the tops follow the slope of the railing. Trim one or both post tops to height, if necessary.

Building a screened-in porch is a very popular do-it-yourself project because the construction techniques are simple, the materials cost is low, and the benefits high. The project shown above is essentially a 2 × 4 stud wall built from floor to ceiling inside the porch rail, with screening material attached.

Screening in Porches

If you have ever built a stud wall and repaired a window screen, you already have most of the skills needed for a screen-in project. A screen-in can be accomplished on many areas of a house or yard, including decks, patios, and gazebos. But by far the most popular area for a screen-in is the front porch. The quick and simple front porch screen-in demonstrated on the following pages is a good example of how to make outdoor living space more livable.

There are many strategies you can take to accomplish a front porch screen-in. If your porch rails and beams are aligned properly, you can convert a plain porch to a screened-in porch

simply by tacking screens to the existing surfaces and installing a screen door. Another easy way to screen in a porch is to build a simple stud wall inside the porch railing, then attach screens to the framework as shown in the following project.

Everything You Need:

Tools: basic hand tools, saws, staple gun, carpenter's level.

Materials: framing lumber, fiberglass insect mesh screening, screen retaining strips, deck screws, brass brads, screen door.

Tips for Planning & Designing a Screened-in Porch

Install kick-guards on the insides of frames to protect the screening. Strips of 1 × 3 or 1 × 4, finished to match the screen frames, often are installed as kick-guards.

Cover gaps between deck boards from below, using retaining strips and brads to tack fiberglass insect mesh to the bottom edges of the floor joists. If you cannot reach the deck boards from below, the best solution is to remove the boards, attach a layer of insect mesh to the tops of the joists, and then reinstall the deck boards.

Options for Screening in a Porch

Build a self-contained frame inside the railings, posts, and beams to support the screening. The self-contained frame is a versatile option that can be used in almost any outdoor structure.

Porches and entryways covered by the main roof of the house often can be screened in simply by attaching the screen materials directly to the existing structure of the porch. Use retaining strips to fasten the screens. Or, check with your local building center to learn more about manufactured screen-in systems. Generally, these systems use rubber spline cords and tracks to secure the screens, allowing the installer to create greater screen tension and reduce the need for screen frames.

How to Screen in Porches

1 Outline the project area on the porch floor, using a chalk line. The goal is to create the largest possible space not obstructed by beams, posts, railings, trim, or the ceiling. Check the corners of the outline with a framing square to make sure the chalk lines are square. Mark the door rough opening—the door width plus 3" for the door frame and ½" for clearance.

2 Attach 2 × 4 sole plates to the porch floor inside the outline, using 3" deck screws driven at 12" intervals. Do not install sole plates in the door rough opening. TIP: If you plan to paint the frames for your screen-in project a different color than the surrounding porch surfaces, paint all of the wood parts for the screen-in before you install them.

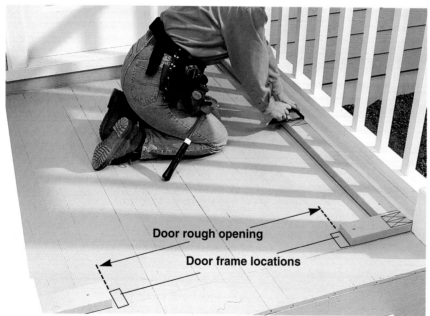

Door rough opening

Door frame locations

3 Mark stud and post locations on the sole plates. Start by marking 2 × 4 door frames at the sides of the door rough opening—frames should rest on the floor, butted against sole plates. Mark doubled 2 × 4 posts at the front corners of the project outline, and mark 2 × 4 end posts on the sole plates next to the wall of the house. Mark 2 × 4 studs for screen supports, spaced at even intervals of 24" to 36", depending on the total distance spanned. Lay 2 × 4 top plates, cut to match the sole plates, next to the sole plates, and copy post and stud marks onto the top plates. The top plate is not cut out for the door opening.

4 Using a straight 2 × 4 and a level, mark the locations for the top plates on the ceiling directly above the sole plates (page 119).

5 Attach the top plates to the ceiling with 3" deck screws driven into joists or beams, if possible. Make sure the top plates are aligned directly above the sole plates, with the framing member marks also in alignment.

6 Cut studs and posts to length, then position and install them at the marks on the top plates and the sole plates. Install by toenailing with 16d galvanized casing nails. When installing the 2 × 4 door frames, nail through the frames and into the ends of the sole plates.

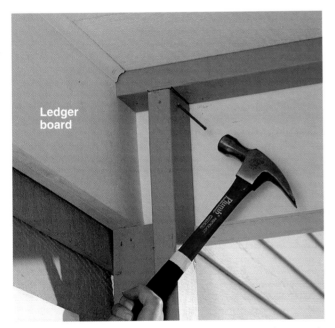

Ledger board

TIP: If the ledger board sticks out past the siding, work around it when installing the 2 × 4 end posts. One solution is to butt two 2 × 4s together so one fits between the floor and the ledger, with the edge against the wall. Toenail the other 2 × 4 into the top plate and sole plate, and nail it to the edge of the first 2 × 4.

7 Cut 2 × 4 spreaders to fit between the studs and posts at the same height as the porch railing. Attach them with 16d casing nails. The spreaders prevent framing members from warping and provide a nailing surface for screen retaining strips.

(continued next page)

How to Screen in Porches (continued)

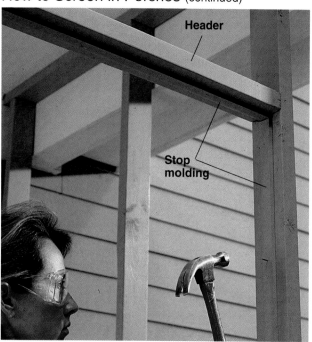

8 Install a 2 × 4 door header to create a rough opening that is ¾" higher than the height of the screen door. Nail door-stop molding to the inside faces of the door frames and header. The stop molding provides surfaces for the door to close against. It should be installed to create a recess the same thickness as the door, so that when it is closed the door is flush with the outside edges of the door frame.

9 Attach hinges to the door. Most screen doors are not prehung, so you will need to buy hinges separately. We used three 2½" door hinges. Install one hinge 12" from the top of the door, and another 12" from the bottom. Space the third evenly between them. Cut a mortise for each hinge into the edge of the door, using a wood chisel, then attach the hinges with wood screws.

10 Set the door in the opening, using ½"-thick spacers to hold it up off the floor. Outline the hinge plates onto the front edge of the door frame.

11 Cut mortises into the door frame at the hinge locations, using a wood chisel. The mortises should be deep enough so the hinge plate will be flush with the surface of the wood. Set the door in the opening, and screw the hinges to the frame.

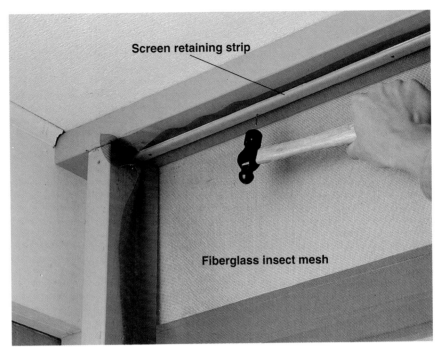

Screen retaining strip

Fiberglass insect mesh

12 Install door hardware, including a door pull, a closer or spring, a wind chain, and a latch or lock if desired. Read the manufacturer's directions for each piece of hardware. OPTION: Install a rubber door sweep on the bottom of the door.

13 Mark centerlines along the inside faces of all studs and posts for reference when installing screens. Using scissors, cut strips of screening so they are at least 4" wider and 4" longer than the opening in the framework where each screen will be installed. Begin attaching screens at the tops of the openings by securing them with wood screen retaining strips. Attach the retaining strips with brass brads spaced at 6" to 12" intervals.

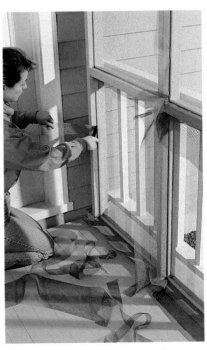

14 With a helper, pull the screen down until taut. Use a retaining strip (cut to the width of the opening) to press the screen against the reference line. Attach the bottom retaining strip near the ends, then staple the screen at the sides, flush against the reference lines. Attach retaining strips at the sides of the opening.

15 Use a utility knife to trim excess screening at the edges of the retaining strips. Install screens in all remaining openings.

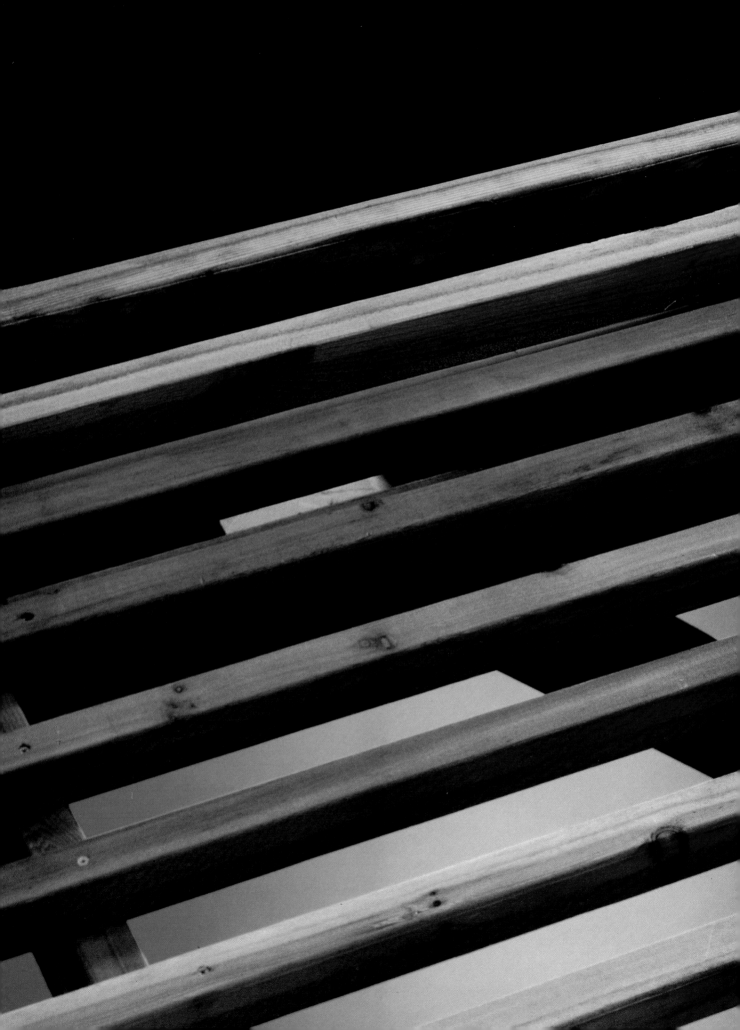

Patio-building Projects

Patios and patio structures are popular do-it-yourself building projects. Some types of patios can be installed easily in one weekend. More complex patios and patio structures, like the sand-set paver patio and three-season porch above, require substantial time and resources, but become the focal point for your outdoor living.

Patio-building Projects

A patio can be as simple as a few square feet of loose rock, or as complex as an expanse of brick pavers mortared over a concrete subbase and surrounded with a wood arbor-and-trellis.

Simple or complex, a patio or patio structure is, first and foremost, meant to be functional. It should provide enough outdoor living space to meet the needs of your family in comfort, with sufficient structural strength and features you will use. A well-designed patio or patio structure also enhances the general appeal of your house and yard.

As with any outdoor building project, begin the patio-building process by evaluating your yard and house, as well as your needs and requirements (pages 12 to 21). When considering a patio, pay special attention to the grade of your yard in and near the building site. If building

next to the house, you may need to do some re-grading to make sure the new patio slopes away from the house slightly. Grading a yard is very important to the long-term success of your project and to the soundness of your house foundation. Always get advice from a landscape designer or a landscape architect before you begin any building project that may alter the drainage patterns of your yard.

This sections shows:

Options for Building Patios & Enclosures

A sand-set paver patio (pages 74 to 83) is easy to install and has an elegant appearance. Pavers are sold in a wide variety of colors, and can be installed in many different patterns. Pavers also can be set in mortar over existing concrete surfaces, provided the surface is in good shape (if not, a new subbase can be poured—see pages 92 to 96).

A poured-concrete patio (pages 84 to 89) is long-lasting and can be built to fit into areas with unusual shapes or sizes. Adding a decorative finish, like the exposed aggregate surface above, introduces new colors and textures into your yard.

A tiled patio surface and an arbor-and-trellis (pages 90 to 103 and 104 to 111) are two projects that can convert a bland patio area into a vibrant and inviting living space.

A patio enclosure (pages 112 to 125) lets you enjoy the outdoors, but still provides shelter. If your existing patio is in good condition, you can build an enclosure around it. Or, you can build a new patio that is fully integrated into the patio-enclosure design.

Building a Paver Patio

Paver patios are built with brick or concrete pavers that are either set loose into a sand base (called sand-set) or set into a bed of mortar. For most homeowners, the sand-set variety is much easier to install. And because the pavers are not permanently bonded, there is little risk of cracking. If pavers do shift, repairing them is as easy as lifting them up, adding or removing sand, and replacing them.

Pavers, whether made of cast concrete or fired brick, are much denser than standard building bricks or blocks. Because of their density, they can be difficult to cut. Try to design a paver patio that requires little or no cutting. If you do need cut pavers, have them cut to size at the brickyard where you make the purchase.

Everything You Need:

Tools: tape measure, carpenter's level, shovel, line level, rake, hand tamper, tamping machine.

Materials: stakes, mason's string, compactible gravel subbase, rigid plastic edging, landscape fabric, sand, pavers, 1"-thick pipes.

Interlocking brick pavers come in many shapes and colors. Two popular paver styles include Uni-Decor™ (left) and Symmetry™ (right). Patios made with interlocking pavers may have a border row made from standard brick pavers (page opposite).

Common Paving Patterns for Standard Brick Pavers

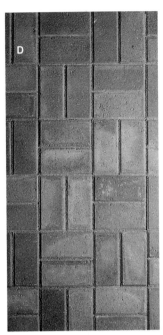

Standard brick pavers can be arranged in several different patterns, including: (A) running bond, (B) jack-on-jack, (C) herringbone, and (D) basket-weave. Jack-on-jack and basketweave patterns require fewer cut pavers along the edges. Know your project dimensions before you order materials, so the salesperson can help you establish exactly how many pavers you will need.

Installation Variations for Brick Pavers

Sand-set: Pavers rest on a 1" bed of sand laid over a 4" compactible gravel subbase (sometimes called "Class 5"). Rigid plastic edging holds the sand in place. Joints are ⅛" wide, and are packed with sand, which holds the pavers securely yet allows them to shift slightly as temperatures change.

Dry mortar: Installation is similar to sand-set patio, but joints are ⅜" wide, and are packed with a mixture of sand and mortar, soaked with water, and finished with a V-shaped mortar tool. A dry-mortar patio has a more finished masonry look than a sand-set patio, but the joints must be repaired periodically.

Wet mortar: This method often is used when pavers are installed over a concrete patio. It is similar to installing patio tiles (pages 90 to 103). Joints are ½" wide. Wet mortar installation can also be used with flagstone. For edging on a wet-mortar patio, use rigid plastic edging or paver bricks set on end.

How to Build a Paver Patio

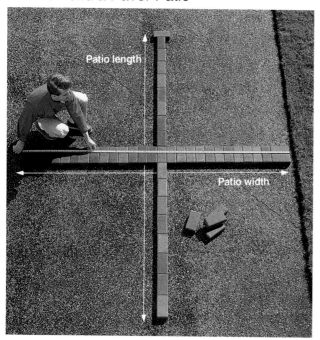

1 To find exact patio measurements and reduce the number of cut bricks needed, test-fit perpendicular rows of brick pavers on a flat surface, like a driveway. Lay two rows to reach the rough length and width of your patio, then measure the rows to find the exact size. (For a dry-mortar patio, put ⅜" spaces between pavers when test-fitting the rows.)

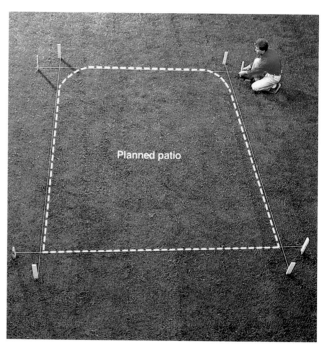

2 Use stakes and mason's string to mark out a rectangle that matches the length and width of your patio. Drive the stakes so they are at least 1 ft. outside the site of the planned patio. The intersecting strings mark the actual corners of the patio site.

3 Check the rectangle for squareness by measuring the diagonals between opposite corners. If the corners are square, the diagonals will have the same measurement. If not, adjust the stakes and strings until the diagonals are equal. The strings will serve as a reference for excavating the patio site.

4 Using a line level as a guide, adjust one of the strings until it is level. When the string is level, mark its height on the stakes at each end of the string.

5 To adjust each remaining string so it is level and even with the first string, use a carpenter's level as a guide for marking adjacent stakes, then adjust the strings to the reference marks. Use a line level to make sure all strings are level.

6 To ensure good drainage, choose one end of the patio as the low end. (For most patios, this will be the end farthest from the house.) Measure from the high end to the low end (in feet), then multiply this number by ⅛" to find the proper drop distance. Measure down from the level marks on the low-end stakes, and mark the drop distance (inset).

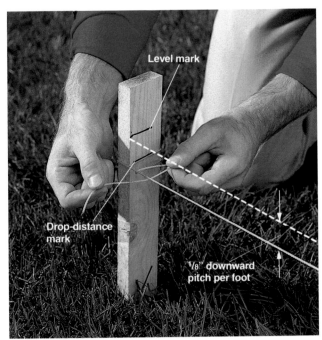

7 Lower the strings at the low-end stakes so the strings are even with the drop-distance marks. Keep all strings in place as a guide while excavating the site and installing the edging.

8 Remove all sod inside the strings and 6" beyond the edges of the planned patio. NOTE: If your patio will have rounded corners, use a garden hose or rope to outline the excavation area.

(continued next page)

9 Starting at the outside edge, excavate the patio site so it is at least 5" deeper than the thickness of the pavers. For example, if your pavers are 1¾" thick, excavate to a depth of 6¾". Try to follow the slope of the side strings, and periodically use a long 2 × 4 to check the bottom of the excavation site for high and low spots.

10 Pour compactible gravel subbase over the patio site, then rake it into a smooth layer at least 4" deep. The thickness of the subbase layer may vary to compensate for unevenness in the excavation. Use a long 2 × 4 to check the surface of the subbase for high and low spots, and add or remove compactible gravel as needed.

11 Pack the subbase with a tamper until the surface is firm and flat. Check the slope of the subbase by measuring down from the side strings (step 14). The space between the strings and the subbase should be equal at all points.

12 Cut strips of landscape fabric and lay them over the subbase to prevent weeds from growing up through the patio. Make sure the strips overlap by at least 6".

13 Install rigid plastic edging around the edges of the patio below the reference strings. Anchor the edging by driving galvanized spikes through the predrilled holes and into the subbase. To allow for possible adjustments, drive only enough spikes to keep the edging in place.

14 Check the slope by measuring from the string to the top of the edging at several points. The measurement should be the same at each point. If not, adjust the edging by adding or removing subbase material under the landscape fabric until the edging follows the slope of the strings.

15 For curves and rounded patio corners, use rigid plastic edging with notches on the outside flange. It may be necessary to anchor each section of edging with spikes to hold curved edging in place.

16 Remove the reference strings, then set 1"-thick pipes or wood strips across the patio area, spaced every 6 ft., to serve as depth spacers for laying the sand base.

(continued next page)

17 Lay a 1"-thick layer of sand over the landscape fabric and smooth it out with a garden rake. Sand should just cover the tops of the depth spacers.

18 Water the sand thoroughly, and pack it lightly with a hand tamper.

19 Smooth out the sand to an even layer by resting a long 2 × 4 on the spacers embedded in the sand and drawing the 2 × 4 across the spacers using a sawing motion. Add extra sand to fill footprints and low areas, then water, tamp, and smooth the sand again until it is firmly packed.

20 Remove the embedded spacers along the sides of the patio base, then fill the grooves with sand and pat them smooth with the hand tamper.

21 Lay the first border paver in one corner of the patio. Make sure the paver rests firmly against the rigid plastic edging.

22 Lay the next border paver so it is tight against the previous paver. Set the pavers by tapping them into the sand with a mallet. Thin ridges, called "lugs," on the sides of the pavers set the joint width automatically.

23 Working outward from the corner, install 2-ft.-wide sections of border pavers and interior pavers, following the desired pattern. Keep surfaces even and joints tight. Set each paver by tapping it with the mallet.

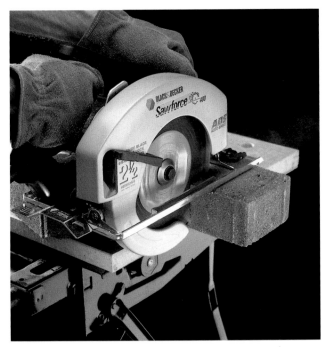

24 If your patio pattern requires that you cut pavers, use a circular saw with a diamond-tipped blade or masonry blade to saw them to size. Always wear eye protection and work gloves when cutting pavers. For big jobs, have the brickyard cut the pavers to size for you.

25 After each section of pavers is set, use a straightedge to make sure the pavers are flat. Make adjustments by tapping high pavers deeper into the sand, or by removing low pavers and adding a thin layer of extra sand underneath them.

(continued next page)

How to Build a Paver Patio (continued)

26 Remove the remaining spacers when the installed surface gets near to them. Fill the gaps left by the spacers with loose sand, and pat the surface smooth with a hand tamper (inset).

27 Continue installing 2-ft.-wide sections of border pavers and interior pavers. As you approach the opposite side of the patio, reposition the rigid plastic edging, if necessary, so full-sized pavers will fit without cutting.

28 At rounded corners and curves, install border pavers in a fan pattern with even gaps between the pavers. Gentle curves may accommodate full-sized border pavers, but for sharper bends you may need to mark and trim wedge-shaped border pavers to make them fit.

29 Lay the remaining interior pavers. Where partial pavers are needed, hold a paver over the gap, and mark the cut with a pencil and straightedge. Cut pavers with a circular saw and masonry blade (step 24). After all pavers are installed, drive in the remaining edging spikes and pack soil behind the edging.

30 Use a long 2 × 4 to check the entire patio for flatness. Adjust uneven pavers by tapping high pavers deeper into the sand, or by removing low pavers and adding a thin layer of extra sand underneath them. After adjusting bricks, use a mason's string to check the rows for straightness.

31 Spread a ½" layer of sand over the patio. Use a tamper to compress the entire patio and pack sand into the joints.

32 Sweep up the loose sand, then soak the patio area thoroughly to settle the sand in the joints. Let the surface dry completely. If necessary, repeat step 31 until the gaps between pavers are packed tightly with sand.

Dry-mortar option: For a finished masonry look, install pavers with a ⅜" gap between bricks. Instead of sand, fill gaps with a dry mixture made from 4 parts sand and 1 part dry mortar. After spreading the dry mixture and tamping the patio, sprinkle surface with water. While mortar joints are damp, finish them with a V-shaped mortar tool (shown above). After mortar hardens, scrub pavers with water and a coarse rag.

This four-square patio replaced a small, crumbling slab that had become an eyesore. The new patio combines pressure-treated wood with aggregate to create a natural-looking, durable surface.

Building a Poured-concrete Patio

Enhance your outdoor living space and beautify your yard by adding an attractive concrete patio. Dividing this 10 ft. × 10 ft. area into four even quadrants, separated by permanent forms, created a strong patio. At the same time, it made it possible to complete the project in four easy stages. Each quadrant can be poured, tooled and seeded separately.

Footings are not needed for this project, since we use an isolation joint to separate the patio from the foundation. Do careful preparation work and add a thick subbase of compactible gravel to improve stability and drainage.

Design the patio to be roomy: allow at least 20 sq. feet of patio space for each regular user. Create a gentle slope away from your house (⅛"

per foot is plenty). Do not exceed more than 1" per foot in slope. If you have never worked with poured concrete before, obtain additional information for concrete mixing, pouring, and finishing techniques.

Everything You Need:

Tools: basic hand tools, mason's string, square-end spade, tamper, wheelbarrow, masonry hoe, wood float, concrete edger, garden rake, wire brush, paint roller.

Materials: wood stakes, compactible gravel subbase, 2 × 4s, deck screws, concrete mix, water, seeding aggregate, sheet plastic, exposed-aggregate sealer.

Design Tips for Concrete Patios

Maintain plenty of clearance between the top of the patio and the door threshold. The top of the patio should be at least 2" below the house sill or threshold so the concrete has room to expand without causing damage in the event of frost heave.

Integrate landscaping into the patio design. The exposed-aggregate surface on this patio seems to almost flow into the adjoining greenery and rock garden.

Incorporate steps or retaining walls into the patio. Originally, the yard in the photo above sloped steeply away from the house. By constructing a retaining wall and integrating steps into the wall, the designer of this masonry project was able to fill in the slope and build a patio near the threshold level.

Build a "floating" patio away from the house. Building a patio in a remote location is a good way to create a separate, defined area for entertaining or relaxing. Floating patios can be built in just about any shape or size.

How to Build a Poured-concrete Patio

1 Prepare the building site by removing any existing building materials, like sidewalks or landing areas. Consider the design tips on the previous page and throughout this book, and select a design for your concrete patio.

2 Lay out the rough position of the patio using a rope or hose, then mark the exact layout with stakes and mason's strings. Use the 3-4-5 method (page 32) or measure the diagonals (page 76) to make sure the project area is square. Establish a ⅛" per ft. slope away from the house, if the ground is level.

3 Remove sod and excavate the project area to a consistent depth, using mason's strings attached to the project stakes for reference. Mark the excavation depth onto a piece of scrap lumber (called a "story pole"), and use it to make sure the excavation is a uniform distance from the strings at all points.

4 Create a subbase for the patio by pouring a 5"-thick layer of compactible gravel, then tamping until it is even and 4" thick.

5 Cut brown pressure-treated 2 × 4 boards to build a permanent form frame that outlines the entire patio site. Lay the boards in place, using the mason's strings as guides. Fasten the ends together with 2½" galvanized deck screws. Temporarily stake the forms at 2-ft. intervals. Set a straight 2 × 4 across the side forms, and set a level on top of the 2 × 4 to check the side forms for level. SAFETY TIP: Wear gloves and a particle mask when cutting pressure-treated lumber.

Half-length form boards

Full-length form board

6 Cut and install pressure-treated 2 × 4s to divide the square into quadrants: cut one piece full length, and attach two one-half length pieces to it with screws driven toenail style. Drive 4" deck screws partway into the forms every 12" at inside locations. The portions that stick out will act as tie rods between the poured concrete and the permanent forms. TIP: Protect the tops of the permanent forms by covering them with masking tape.

7 Cut reinforcing wire mesh to fit inside each quadrant, leaving 1" clearance on all sides. Mix concrete and pour the quadrants one at a time, starting with the one located farthest from the concrete source. Use a masonry hoe to spread the concrete evenly in the forms.

8 Smooth off the concrete with a straight 2 × 4 that rests on the forms (called a "screed board"). Settle the concrete by sliding a spade along the inside edges of the forms and rapping the outer edges of the forms with a hammer.

(continued next page)

How to Build a Poured-concrete Patio (continued)

9 After smoothing off the surface, cover the concrete with a full layer of "seeding aggregate." Use a float to embed the aggregate completely into the concrete. NOTE: Seeding aggregate is a mixture of small stones and pebbles sold by most sand and gravel distributors in a range of colors and types.

10 Cut along the edges of the quadrant with a concrete edger, then use a wood float to smooth out any marks left behind by the tool. TIP: If you plan to pour more quadrants immediately, cover the seeded concrete with plastic so it does not dry too quickly.

11 Pour the remaining quadrants, repeating steps 7 through 10. Check poured quadrants periodically; if water has formed on and evaporated from the surface, uncover the quadrants and proceed to step 12.

12 After all the water has evaporated from the concrete surface, expose the aggregate by misting the surface with water and scrubbing the surface with a stiff-bristled brush. Remove the protective tape from the forms, then re-cover the quadrants with plastic and let the concrete cure for one week.

13 After the concrete has cured, rinse and scrub the aggregate again to clean off any remaining residue. TIP: Use diluted muriatic acid to wash off stubborn concrete residue. Read manufacturer's instructions for mixing ratios and safety precautions.

14 Wait three weeks, then seal the patio surface with exposed-aggregate sealer. Reapply sealer periodically as needed, following the manufacturer's recommendations.

Patio tile can turn a drab concrete slab into a charming outdoor living area. To create this tiled project, we first poured a new concrete subbase over an existing concrete patio (inset).

Installing Tiled Patios

If you have ever laid ceramic or vinyl tile inside your house, you already have valuable experience that will help you lay patio tile.

The primary difference between interior and exterior tile is in the thickness of the tiles and the water-absorption rates. The project layout and application techniques are quite similar. With patio tiling projects, however, preparing or creating a suitable subbase for the tiles can become a fairly intensive project. Because any exterior project must stand up to the elements, a sturdy subbase is critical.

Patio tile is most frequently applied over a concrete subbase—either an existing concrete patio, or a new concrete slab. A third option, which we show you on the following pages, is to pour a new tile subbase over an existing concrete patio. This option involves far less work and expense than removing an old patio and pouring a new slab. And it ensures that your new tiled patio will not develop the same problems that

may be present in the existing concrete surface. See the photographs at the top of page 92 to help you determine the best method for preparing an existing concrete patio for tile.

If you do not have a concrete slab in the project area already, you will need to pour one before you tile (see *Home Masonry Repairs & Projects,* Black & Decker® Home Improvement Library™).

The patio tiling project shown here is divided into two separate projects: pouring a new subbase, and installing patio tile. If your existing patio is in good condition, you do not need to pour a new subbase.

When selecting tiles for your patio, make sure the product you purchase is exterior tile, which is designed to better withstand freezing and thawing than interior tile. Try to select colors and textures that match or complement other parts of your house and yard. If your project requires extensive tile cutting, arrange to have the tiles cut to size at the supply center.

Exterior tile products for patios are denser and thicker than interior tile. Common types include shell-stone tile, ceramic patio tile, and quarry tile. The most common size is 12" × 12", but you also can purchase precut designer tiles that are assembled into elaborate patterns and designs.

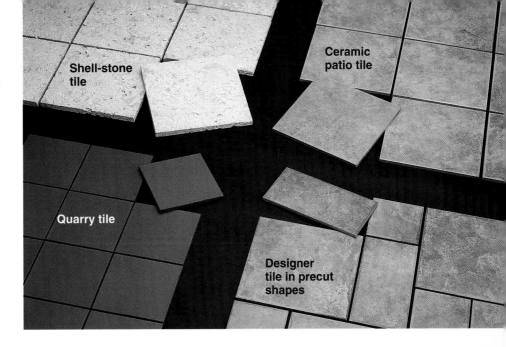

Tools for working with exterior tile include: a wet saw for cutting large amounts of tile (usually a rental item); a square-notched trowel for spreading tile adhesive; a grout float for spreading grout into joints between tiles; a sponge for wiping up excess grout; tile nippers for making curved or angled cuts in tiles; tile spacers to set standard joints between tiles; and a rubber mallet for setting tiles into adhesive.

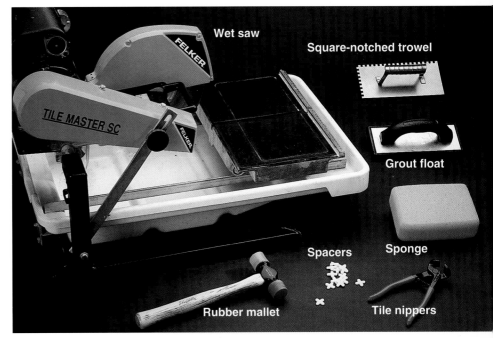

Materials for installing patio tile include: exterior tile grout (tinted or untinted); acrylic grout sealer; latex caulk for filling tile joints over control joints; caulk backer rod to keep grout out of control joints during grout application; latex-fortified grout additive; tile sealer; concrete floor-mix for building a tile subbase; tile adhesive (dry-set mortar); and a mortar bag for filling joints with grout (optional).

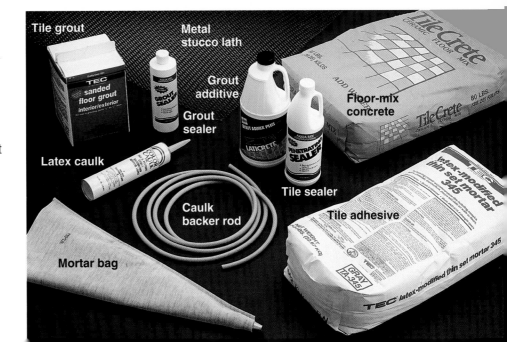

Tips for Evaluating Concrete Surfaces

A good surface is free from any major cracks or badly flaking concrete (called spalling). You can apply patio tile directly over a concrete surface that is in good condition if it has control joints (see below).

A fair surface may exhibit minor cracking and spalling, but has no major cracks or badly deteriorated spots. Install a new concrete subbase over a surface in fair condition before laying patio tile.

A poor surface contains deep or large cracks, broken, sunken or heaved concrete, or extensive spalling. If you have this kind of surface, remove the concrete completely and replace it with a new concrete slab before you lay patio tile.

Tips for Cutting Control Joints in a Concrete Patio

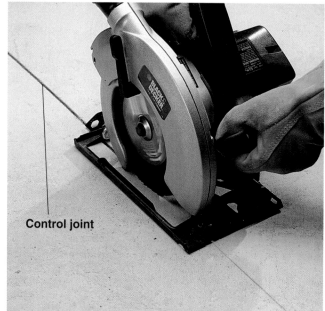 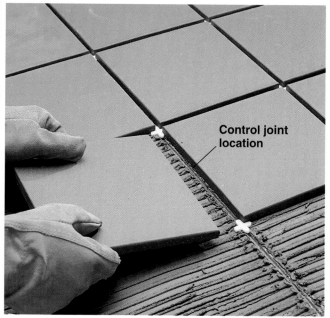

Cut new control joints into existing concrete patios that are in good condition (see above) but do not have enough control joints—control joints manage cracking in concrete by directing cracks in directions that do not weaken the concrete or detract from the appearance. They should be cut every 5 or 6 ft. in a patio. Use a circular saw with a masonry blade set to ⅜" depth to cut control joints. If possible, plan the control joints so they will be below tile joints once the tile layout is established.

How to Install a Subbase for Patio Tile

Pour a layer of floor-mix concrete over an old concrete patio to create a level tile subbase free from cracks that can cause new tile to fail.

Pouring a concrete subbase over an old concrete slab is similar to other concrete projects, but with a few important differences. As with most projects, you will need to: install wooden forms around the perimeter of the project area, smooth the concrete surface, and cure the concrete.

Elements unique to this project include: the use of floor-mix concrete (a dry mix designed for pouring a subbase), the need for a bond-breaker (we laid 30# building paper over the old surface to keep the new surface from adhering to it), and special reinforcement requirements (we used ⅜"-thick metal stucco lath).

Everything You Need:

Tools: basic hand tools, shovel, maul, straight-edge, masonry hoe, mortar box, tamper, magnesium float, concrete edger, utility knife, trowel.

Materials: 30# building paper, sheet plastic, 2 × 4 lumber, stucco lath, tile subbase, floor mix, roofing cement.

Form braces
2 × 4 form boards

1 Dig a trench around the old patio to create room for 2 × 4 forms. Make the trench at least 6" wide, and no more than 4" deep. Clean all dirt and debris from the exposed sides of the patio. Cut 2 × 4s the same length as the sides of the patio, then measure the side-to-side distance, add 3" to the length of the side forms, and cut 2 × 4s for the front—and for the back if the patio is not next to the house. Lay 2 × 4s around the patio, on edge, and join the ends with 3" deck screws. Cut several 12"-long wood stakes and drive them next to the forms, at 2-ft. intervals.

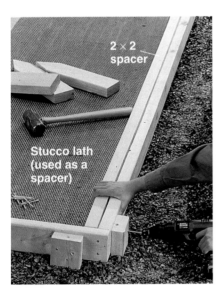

2 × 2 spacer

Stucco lath (used as a spacer)

2 Adjust form height: set a stucco lath spacer on the surface, then set a 2 × 2 spacer on top of the lath (their combined thickness equals the thickness of the subbase). Adjust the tops of the form boards so they are level with the 2 × 2 spacer, and screw the braces to the forms.

Building paper "bond-breaker"

3 Remove the spacers, then lay strips of 30# building paper over the old patio surface, overlapping seams by 6", to create a "bond-breaker" for the new surface (this prevents the new subbase from bonding directly to the old concrete). Crease the building paper at the edges and corners, making sure the paper extends past the tops of the forms. Make a small cut in the paper at each corner so the paper can be folded over more easily.

(continued next page)

Screed board

4 Lay strips of stucco lath over the building-paper bond-breaker, overlapping seams by 1". Keep the lath 1" away from forms and the wall. Use aviator snips to cut the stucco lath (wear heavy gloves when handling metal).

5 Install temporary 2 × 2 forms to divide the project into working sections and provide rests for the "screed board" used to level and smooth the fresh concrete. Make the sections narrow enough that you can reach across the entire section (3-ft. to 4-ft. sections are comfortable for most people). Screw the ends of the 2 × 2s to the form boards so the tops are level.

6 Mix dry floor-mix concrete with water in a mortar box, blending with a masonry hoe, according to the manufacturer's directions. The mixture should be very dry when prepared (inset) so it can be pressed down into the voids in the stucco lath with a tamper.

7 Fill one working section with floor-mix concrete, up to the tops of the forms. Tamp the concrete thoroughly with a lightweight tamper to help force it into the voids in the lath and into corners. The lightweight tamper shown above is made from a 12" × 12" piece of ¾" plywood, with a 2 × 4 handle attached.

8 Level off the surface of the concrete by dragging a straight 2 x 4 "screed board" across the top, with the ends riding on the forms. Move the 2 x 4 in a sawing motion as you progress. Called "screeding" or "striking-off," this process creates a level surface and fills any voids in the concrete. If any voids or hollows remain, add more concrete and smooth it off.

9 Use a wood float to smooth out the surface of the concrete. Applying very light pressure, move the float back and forth in an arching motion, tipping the lead edge up slightly to avoid gouging the surface. Float the surface a second time, using a magnesium float, to create a hard, smooth surface.

10 Pour and smooth out the next working section, repeating steps 7 to 9. After floating this section, remove the 2 x 2 temporary form between the two sections. Fill the void left behind with fresh concrete. Float the fresh concrete with the magnesium float until it is smooth, level, and it blends into the working section on each side. Pour and finish the remaining working sections one at a time, using the same techniques.

(continued next page)

How to Install a Subbase for Patio Tile (continued)

11 Let the concrete dry until pressing the surface with your finger does not leave a mark. Cut contours around all edges of the subbase with a concrete edger. Tip the lead edge of the edger up slightly to avoid gouging the surface. Smooth out any marks left by the edger, using a float.

12 Cover the concrete subbase with sheets of plastic, and cure for at least three days (see manufacturer's directions for recommended curing time). Weight down the edges of the sheeting. After curing is compete, remove the plastic and disassemble and remove the forms.

13 Trim off the building paper around the sides of the patio, using a utility knife. Apply plastic roof cement to the sides of the patio with a putty knife or trowel, to fill and seal the seam between the old sur- face and the new surface. To provide drainage for moisture between layers, do not seal the lowest side of the patio. After the roof cement dries, shovel dirt or groundcover back into the trench around the patio.

Installing Tiled Patios

How to Lay Patio Tile

With any tiling project, the most important part of the job is creating and marking the layout lines and pattern for the tile. The best way to do this is to perform a dry run using the tiles you will install. Try to find a layout that requires the least possible amount of cutting.

Once you have established an efficient layout plan, carefully mark square reference lines in the project area. Creating a professional-looking tiled patio requires that you follow the lines and use sound installation techniques.

Some patio tile is fashioned with small ridges on the edges that automatically establish the spacing between tiles. But more often, you will need to insert plastic spacers between tiles as you work. The spacers should be removed before the tile adhesive dries.

Tiled patios are vulnerable to cracking. Make sure the tile subbase has sufficient control joints to keep cracking in check (page 92). Install tiles so the control joints are covered by tile joints. Fill the tile joints over the control joints with flexible latex caulk, not grout.

Everything You Need:

Tools: carpenter's square, straightedge, tape measure, chalk line, tile cutter, tile nippers, tile spacers, trowel, rubber mallet, grout float, grout sponge, caulk gun.

Materials: buckets, paint brush and roller, plastic sheeting, paper towels, dry-set mortar, tile, backer rod, grout, grout additive, grout chalk, grout sealer, tile sealer.

1 Without applying adhesive, set rows of tile onto the surface so they run in each direction, intersecting in the center of the patio. Slip tile spacers between tiles to represent joints (inset). This "dry lay" helps you establish and mark an attractive, efficient layout for the tile.

2 Adjust the dry lay to create a layout that minimizes tile cutting. Shift the rows of tiles and spacers until the overhang is equal at each end, and any cut portions are less than 2" wide. Note: Tiles should be ¼" to ½" away from the house.

Snap chalk line for reference

3 Once the layout is set, mark layout lines onto the tiling surface. Mark the surface at the joint between the third and fourth row out from the house, then measure the distance and mark it at several more points along the project area. Snap a chalk line to connect the marks.

(continued next page)

4 Use a carpenter's square and a long, straight board to mark end points for a second reference line perpendicular to the first. Mark the points next to the dry-laid tile so the line falls on a joint location. Remove tools and tiles, and snap a chalkline that connects the points.

5 Lay tiles in one quadrant at a time, beginning with a section next to the house. Start by mixing a batch of dry-set mortar in a bucket, according to the manufacturer's directions. Spread mortar evenly along both legs of one quadrant, using a square-notched trowel. Apply enough mortar for four tiles along each leg.

6 Use the edge of the trowel to create furrows in the mortar. Make sure you have applied enough mortar to completely cover the area under the tiles, without covering up the reference lines.

7 Set the first tile in the corner of the quadrant where the lines intersect, pressing down lightly and twisting slightly from side to side. Adjust the tile until it is exactly aligned with both reference lines.

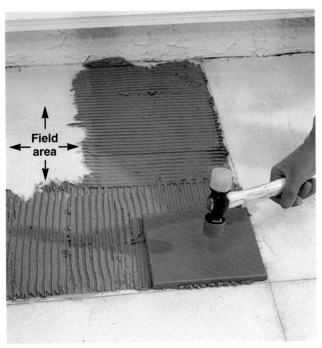

Field area

8 Rap the tile gently with a rubber mallet to set it into the mortar. Rap evenly across the entire surface area, being careful not to break the tile or completely displace the mortar beneath the tile. NOTE: Once you start to fill in the "field" area of the quadrant, it is faster to place several tiles at once, then set them all with the mallet at one time.

9 Set plastic spacers at the corner of the tile that faces the working quadrant. NOTE: Plastic spacers are only temporary: be sure to remove them before the mortar hardens—usually within one hour.

10 Position the next tile into the mortar bed along one arm of the quadrant, making sure the tiles fit neatly against the spacers. Rap the tile with the mallet to set it into the mortar, then position and set the next tile on the other leg of the quadrant. Make certain the tiles align with the reference lines.

11 Fill out the rest of the tile in the mortared area of the quadrant, using the spacers to maintain uniform joints between tiles. Wipe off any excess mortar before it dries.

(continued next page)

12 Apply a furrowed layer of mortar to the field area: do not cover more area than you can tile in 15 to 20 minutes. TIP: Start with smaller sections, then increase the size as you get a better idea of your working pace.

13 Set tiles into the field area of the first quadrant, saving any cut tiles for last. Rent a wet saw from your local rental store for cutting tiles, or have them cut to size. To save time, have all tiles cut before you start laying tiles.

14 Apply mortar and fill in tiles in the next quadrant against the house, using the same techniques used for the first quadrant. Carefully remove plastic spacers with a screwdriver as you finish each quadrant—do not leave spacers in mortar for more than one hour.

15 Fill in the remaining quadrants. TIP: Use a straightedge to check the tile joints occasionally. If you find that any of the joint lines are out of alignment, compensate for the misalignment over several rows of tiles.

16 After all the tiles for the patio are set, check to make sure all spacers are removed and any excess mortar has been cleaned from the tile surfaces. Cover the project area with plastic for three days to allow the mortar to cure properly.

Caulking backer rod

17 After three days, remove the plastic and prepare the tile for "grouting" (the process of filling the joints between tiles with grout). Create expansion joints on the tiled surface by inserting strips of ¼"-diameter caulking backer rod into the joints between quadrants, and over any control joints (page 92), to keep grout out of these joints.

(continued next page)

18 Mix a batch of tile grout to the recommended consistency. TIP: Add latex-fortified grout additive so excess grout is easier to remove. Starting in a corner and working out, pour a layer of grout onto an area of the surface that is 25 square feet or less in size. Spread out the grout with a rubber grout float so it completely fills the joints between tiles.

19 Use the grout float to scrape off excess grout from the surface of the tile. Scrape diagonally across the joints, holding the float in a near-vertical position. Patio tile will absorb grout quickly and permanently, so it is important to remove all excess grout from the surface before it sets.

20 Use a damp sponge to wipe the grout film from the surface of the tile. Rinse the sponge out frequently with cool water, and be careful not to press down so hard around joints that you disturb the grout. Wash grout off of the entire surface.

21 Let the grout dry for about four hours, then test by poking with a nail to make sure it is completely hardened. Use a cloth to buff the surface of the tile until all remaining grout film is gone. If buffing does not remove all the film, try using a coarser cloth, like burlap, or even an abrasive pad to remove stubborn grout film.

22 Remove the caulking backer rods from the tile joints, then fill the joints with caulk that is tinted to match the grout color closely. The caulk will allow for some expansion and contraction of the tiled surface, preventing cracking and buckling.

23 Apply grout sealer to the grout lines using a sash brush or small sponge brush. Avoid spilling over onto the tile surface with the grout sealer. Wipe up any spills immediately.

24 OPTION: After one to three weeks, seal the tiled surface with tile sealer, following the manufacturer's application directions. A paint roller with an extension pole is a good tool for applying tile or concrete sealer.

Arbor structures make a dramatic visual statement when constructed over an ordinary patio. They also help cut down on wind and sun, and create a more pleasant outdoor environment. See pages 110 to 111 for information on adding a trellis to an arbor.

Building Arbor Structures

An arbor is an overhead system of beams, usually supported by posts, that provides shade and is often used to train climbing plants. Arbors can be built as independent yard structures, but they often are combined with a trellis—a lattice wall attached to the side of the arbor (pages 110 to 111). The combined arbor-and-trellis is a traditional, attractive outdoor structure.

Build your arbor structure so it is freestanding— do not attach it directly to your house. A permanent structure that is attached to a house must meet more code requirements than freestanding structures, and there is more risk of structural failure. The arbor featured in this section is made with four-post construction, set on sturdy concrete footings. Because it is freestanding, the

footings did not need to extend below the frost line (page 16). Very small garden arbors can be built with techniques and materials similar to those used for the project shown, but may not require post footings.

Everything You Need:

Tools: tape measure, mason's string, line level, torpedo level, carpenter's square, speed square, drill, circular saw, ratchet-socket set, ladder, shovel, mortar box.

Materials: concrete, cedar framing lumber, isolation boards, post anchors, carriage bolts, lag screws, rafter ties, deck screws, J-bolts.

Design Tips

Build an arbor over an entry point to your house to create shade and dress up a plain entry. An arbor can be built over an entry stoop or stairs, on a deck, or over a patio.

Build a freestanding arbor on a deck or patio, or in a remote area of your yard. A simple arbor like the one shown above can turn a forgotten area into an intimate setting that may become your favorite outdoor relaxation spot.

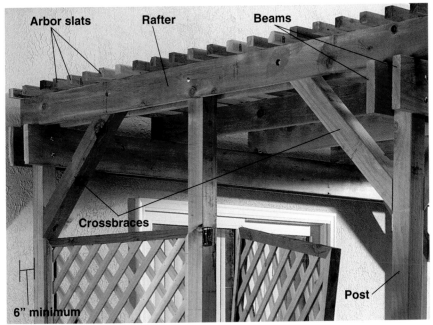

Arbor slats   Rafter   Beams

Crossbraces

6" minimum

Post

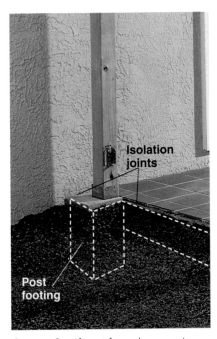

Isolation joints

Post footing

Build an independent post framework—a better option for arbors than tying them to your house with a ledger board, as you would a more permanent structure. Make sure that posts are at least 6" away from the house so you will have enough room to attach the beams to the posts. Larger arbor structures should have cross-bracing that joins the posts and beams. Attach the cross braces with lag screws driven into the posts. Depending on the structure of your beams, you may be able to attach the cross brace between doubled rafters (as shown above). Otherwise, lag-screw cross braces to the posts and to the beams.

Create footings for arbor posts, according to local building code requirements. Use building paper or fiberboard to form isolation joints between the footings and foundations and concrete patio slabs. In some cases, footings may be required to extend below the frost line.

How to Build Arbors

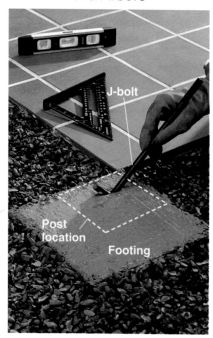

1 Create footings for the arbor posts by digging a hole at least twice the size of the post bottom and at least 12" deep. Fill with concrete, and set a J-bolt in each concrete footing. We positioned the J-bolts so the edges of the posts are flush with the patio.

2 Allow the footings to harden for at least one day, then attach post anchor hardware to the J-bolts (page 34). Cut and install arbor posts—for most arbors, 4 × 4 posts are large enough. Cut posts slightly longer than the planned height, and brace them with 2 × 4 braces so they are plumb. Leave the braces in place until the beams and rafters are secured in position.

3 Use a square to mark cutting lines for the posts at the desired height: mark the height of the arbor onto the posts at one end, then use a line level to transfer the height mark onto the posts at the other end. With a square, mark cutting lines on all four sides of each post. Trim the posts at the cutting lines,

using a handsaw. Have a helper steady the post from below while you cut. NOTE: You may use a power saw, like a reciprocating saw, to cut off post tops, but only if your ladder provides enough elevation that you can work from above the cutting line.

4 Cut beam members from 2 × 8 stock. Because we used two beam members each at the front and back of the project, we cut four beam members. To create a 6" overhang at each side, we cut the beam members 12" longer than the distance between the outside edges of the posts. Mark all beam members with a carpenter's square, then gang-cut them with a circular saw and straightedge.

5 Turn beams on edge, and mark locations for rafters. Rafters should be no more than 24" apart. Start by marking the outermost rafters—our plan called for a rafter at the inside and outside edge of each post. Do not forget to include the beam overhang in the layout.

Outer rafter locations
Post location
Beam overhang

Guide strip

6 Fasten the beam members to the posts at the front and back of the arbor. Screw a guide strip securely to the top of each post, then position the beam members and hold them in place temporarily by driving a screw down through the guide strip and into the top of each beam member. When installing beam pairs, as shown here, use a pair of carriage bolts with washers and nuts at each beam/post joint. Attach a ½" bit with a bit extension to your drill, and drill holes for the carriage bolts through both beam members and the post, counterboring for the nuts and washers that will be visible.

(continued next page)

7 Pound ½"-diameter carriage bolts through the holes. Carriage bolts should be ½" to 1" longer than the combined widths of the outer rafters and the beam—for this project, we used a 7"-long bolt. Slip a washer and nut onto the end of the carriage bolt, and tighten with a ratchet. Remove the guide strip.

8 Measure and mark 2 × 6 rafters to fit on top of the beams, perpendicular to the house. Mark the full length on each rafter. For best appearance, rafters should overhang the beams by at least 6". Cut with a circular saw. For added visual appeal, mark an angled cut of about 30° at the end of one rafter, then cut off with a circular saw. Use the rafter as a template to transfer the angle to the other rafters.

Rafter tie

9 Install rafters on top of the beams at the rafter layout marks. Position the rafters so the angled ends are at the front of the project, with the shorter side resting on the beam. Use metal rafter ties, mounted to the beams, and deck screws to attach the rafters. OPTION: Because the metal rafter ties can be quite visible in the finished product, you may prefer to toe-nail the rafters in place with 16d galvanized nails.

Beam mark

Cross-brace location

18"

18"

Post mark

10 Mark posts and beams for cross braces. From the inside corner of each post/beam joint, mark an equal distance (about 18") on the beam and the post. For cross braces that fit between rafters, measure from the post mark to the top of the rafter, following the line created between the post mark and the beam mark. For cross braces that fit flush with the post and the beam, measure from post mark to beam mark for the inside dimension of the cross brace.

11 Mark the inside dimensions for the cross braces (step 10) onto a piece of lumber of the same type as the posts (here, 4 × 4). Use a square or triangle to draw 45° cutting lines away from each end point of the inside dimension. Cut along these lines with a circular saw to make the cross braces.

12 Install cross braces. Tack the cross braces in position, then attach with ⅜" × 4" lag screws. If the cross brace is fitted between rafters, drive lag screws through counterbored pilot holes in the rafter, and into the cross brace at the top. Attach at flush joints with two lag screws at each joint. Drive lag screws through counterbored pilot holes that are perpendicular to the post or rafter.

13 Install arbor slats on top of the rafters, using 2½" deck screws. We used 2 × 2 cedar spaced at 4" intervals. Include an overhang of at least 6". Attach the arbor slats with 2½" deck screws driven down through the slats and into the rafters.

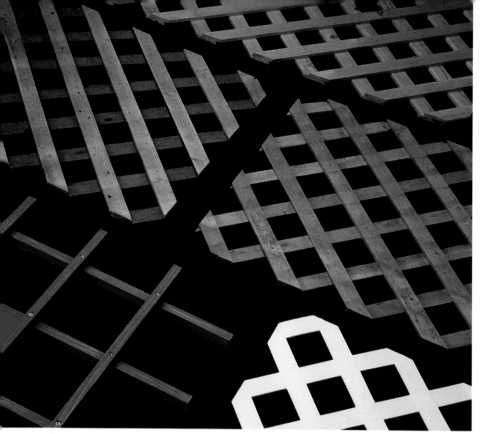

Adding a Trellis to an Arbor

Add a lattice-panel trellis to an arbor structure for a more decorative appearance. Using manufactured lattice panels and lattice molding, and hanging the panels with metal fence-panel hangers, makes the job inexpensive and quick. Or, you can build your own lattice and frame. Plant climbing plants and train them up the trellis to embellish the arbor-and-trellis.

Lattice panels are used to create the trellis portion of an arbor-and-trellis. Most building centers carry cedar, pressure-treated, and vinyl lattice in 2-ft. × 8-ft. and 4-ft. × 8-ft. panels. Standard lattice panels are ¾" thick. For a more customized look, you can build your own lattice panels from exterior-rated lumber.

Everything You Need:

Tools: pencil, tape measure, circular saw, chalk line, hammer, drill.

Materials: 4 × 8 lattice panels, lattice molding, galvanized brads, fence brackets.

How to Add a Trellis to an Arbor

1 If the planned trellis is wider than 4 ft., you will need additional support posts. Install posts using the same materials and techniques used for the corner posts of the arbor (page 106). If possible, install the posts so the lattice panels on either side of each post will be equal in size.

2 Measure the openings between the posts to determine the sizes for the lattice panels. Generally, panels should be sized so they are installed below the cross braces between posts. Leave a few inches of open space beneath the panels at ground level. Mark the locations of the panel tops onto the posts, using a level to make sure the tops are even.

3 Subtract 1½" from the frame opening dimensions, and cut the lattice panels to size. To cut lattice panels, sandwich each panel between two boards near the cutting line to prevent the lattice from separating. Clamp the boards and the panel together and cut with a circular saw.

4 Miter-cut 2 × 2 lattice molding to frame the lattice panels. The finished width of the panel should be ½" narrower than the opening. Nail one vertical and one horizontal frame piece together with galvanized brads. Set the lattice panel into the channels, add attach the other frame pieces. Secure the lattice panels into the molding by driving brads through the molding and into the lattice at 12" intervals.

5 Attach three fence brackets to the posts, evenly spaced, on each side of the opening, using 4d galvanized nails. On the top two brackets, bend the bottom and top flanges flat against the post. Bend all outside flanges flat.

6 Set the panels in the brackets, and bend the hanger flanges back to their original positions. Drive 1" galvanized nails through the flanges of the fence hangers and into the frames of the lattice panels.

A patio enclosure offers the benefits of a permanent structure, but it can be built with inexpensive outdoor building materials using only basic rough carpentry skills. The patio enclosure above was built around the tiled patio project shown in pages 90 to 103.

Before

After

Building Patio Enclosures

A patio enclosure is any structure built around a patio to completely block out wind and rain. Typically, they are unheated and uninsulated, and electrical access is limited to exterior receptacles on the walls of the house.

The project shown on the following pages is a typical patio enclosure project. It is likely that your enclosure project will differ to some degree from the project shown here. But whatever the design of your own project, read this information carefully to gain a better understanding of the challenges you will encounter and to learn how those challenges can be addressed.

Be sure to check with your local building inspector before you begin the project to learn about construction codes and permits. It is always a good idea to work with a professional designer or architect to create a detailed construction plan.

This project shows:
• How to Install Footings, Posts & Roofs (pages 114 to 118)
• How to Install Walls, Windows & Doors (pages 119 to 123)
• How to Install Wall Coverings & Trim (pages 124 to 125)

Anatomy of a Patio Enclosure

Most patio enclosure structures have three basic elements: the foundation and the floor; the walls, windows and doors; and the roof system. Of these, the roof system is the most challenging element for the do-it-yourselfer. There are a variety of patio roof products to choose from, but one of the most economical solutions is to install a corrugated roof panel system (page 114). Corrugated panel systems are installed over a network of rafters and spacers, called "purlins." The rafters can be tricky to install because they must be trimmed at an angle where they meet the house. If the cutting angle for the rafters is not indicated on your construction plan, consult an engineer or a building construction reference book to find the required angle.

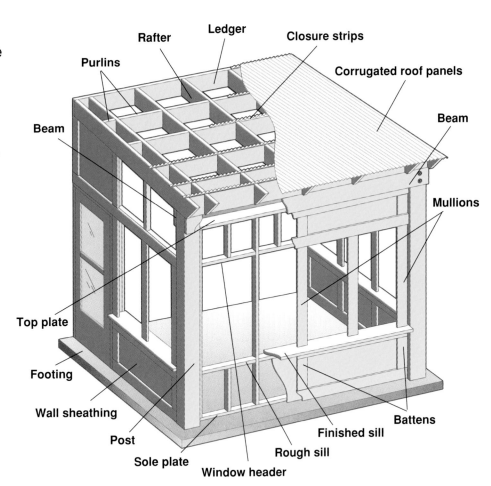

Labels: Rafter, Ledger, Closure strips, Purlins, Corrugated roof panels, Beam, Beam, Mullions, Top plate, Footing, Wall sheathing, Battens, Post, Finished sill, Sole plate, Rough sill, Window header

Tips for Planning a Patio Enclosure Project

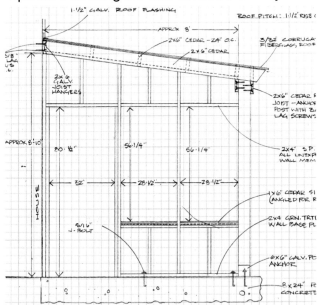

Work from a blueprint or plan. Consult a professional architect or designer to help you design a project that meets your needs (pages 12 to 17). Working from approved plans that are created with professional input is a key factor in the success of any patio enclosure project.

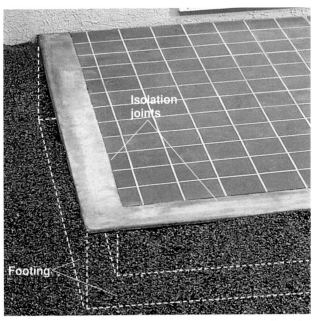

Isolation joints

Footing

Create footings for the patio enclosure walls. Check with your building department for code requirements. One way to create a footing for walls is to dig a trench around the concrete slab, to the required width and depth. Pour concrete into the trench, using building paper or fiberboard to form an isolation joint that keeps the footing from bonding to the old concrete. If you do not have experience working with concrete, get additional information before you start.

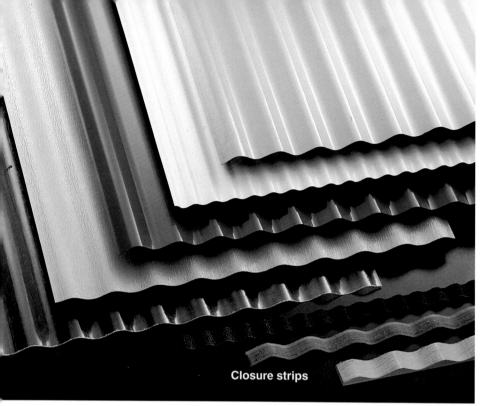

Closure strips

How to Install Footings, Posts & Roofs

The footings, posts, and roof system are the primary structural parts of a patio enclosure. When building an enclosure around an existing concrete patio, install frost footings for the wall that are isolated from the patio so they move independently. The posts rest on the footings to support beams and the rest of the roof system.

Corrugated roof systems are inexpensive and easy to construct with corrugated roof panels made of fiberglass or PVC. Sold in a variety of colors and transparencies, fiberglass panels are more rigid and let in more light than PVC panels. PVC panels are available in a wide selection of colors. Roofing panels are also available in different lengths, so you can cover the roof without creating horizontal seams. All corrugated roofing panels require closure strips that attach to the rafters to close off the space below the peaks in the panels. Use wood closure strips for fiberglass panels, and foam closure strips for PVC panels.

Everything You Need:

Tools: basic hand tools, speed square, caulk gun.

Materials: construction plan, concrete, J-bolts, post anchors, wood posts, framing lumber, joist hangers, roof materials (photo, left), flashing, lag screws, deck screws, nails, caulk.

Planned door location

*J-bolt locations for project as shown

J-bolt

1 Create a frost footing for the patio enclosure walls, around the perimeter of the patio (see photo, above). Before the concrete for the footing dries, use the post locations from your plan as a reference for setting J-bolts into the concrete (inset, and page 34). Install a J-bolt at the centerpoint for each planned post, and at 3-ft. intervals in the area where the sole plates will be attached. Do not set J-bolts at the door location. Let the footing cure for at least three days before installing post anchors.

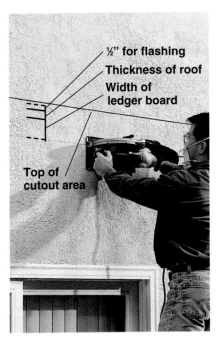

2 Mark a cutout area to remove siding for the ledger board (pages 30 to 32) that will support the rafters and anchor the patio enclosure to your house. Measure up from the patio at both ends of the project area, and mark the height of the patio enclosure, including the thickness of the roof, onto the wall at each end. Add ½" for roof flashing (step 3 photo), then snap a chalkline between the points to mark the top of the cutout area. Add the width of the ledger board, the thickness of the roof, and ½". Measure down that amount from the chalkline, mark points, and snap a chalkline for the bottom of the cutout area. Mark the ends of the cutout area even with the outside faces of the posts in their planned locations.

3 Remove siding in the cutout area (page 15). Attach a 2 × 6 ledger board in the cutout area with 3½" lag screws driven at stud locations. The bottom of the board should be flush with the bottom of the cutout.

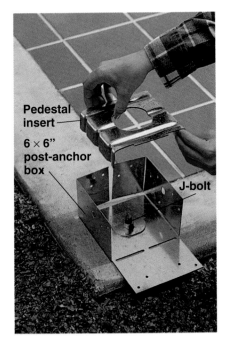

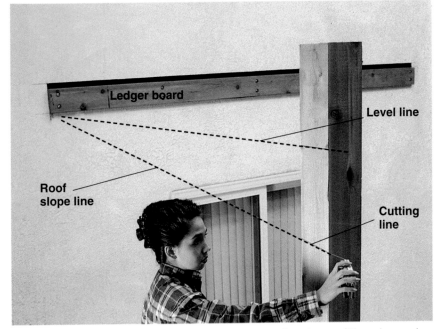

4 Secure post anchors to J-bolts with washers and nuts. NOTE: Post anchors for 6 × 6" posts have a pedestal insert that fits into the anchor box. Cut and install the posts (page 34).

5 Once the ledger and the posts are set, use the slope of the planned roof to mark the tops of the posts for trimming. If your planned roof has a slope of 1½" per foot (as shown above), measure down from the level line on the posts 1½" for every foot of distance between the ledger and the posts. Mark a sloped cutting line across the face of the posts, then cut off posts along this line with a handsaw.

(continued next page)

6 Install the beams. First, cut two 2 × 6 beams the same length as the ledger. Tack a strip of wood to the top of each post as a guide. With a helper, tack a beam to the front of one post with duplex nails, so the ends are flush with the outside face of the post, and the top is pressed up to the guide. Tack the other end. Attach another beam to the backs of the posts, pressed up to the guides. Drill counterbored pilot holes for ½ × 4"-long lag screws, then screw each beam to the posts with two lag screws at each end.

7 Mark and cut the rafters from 2 × 6s, ganged together for marking and cutting. Use a speed square (page 20) to mark the cutting angles for the ends of the rafters where they meet the ledger (see construction plan). Draw a cutting line at the front end of the rafter so the rafter overhangs the front beam by at least ½" (for decorative appeal, angle-cut the front end to match the ledger end). Mark locations for "purlins" between rafters (step 9) on the edges of the rafters, spaced 24" on center.

8 Mark the rafter locations onto the ledger and the tops of the beams, following your construction plans (24" on center is standard). NOTE: To provide a framework for the patio enclosure walls, we installed rafters on both sides of the posts (see step 5, page 120). Install joist hangers with joist-hanger nails at the rafter locations on the ledger. Set the rafters on the beams, with the other ends in the joist hangers. Attach rafters to the joist hangers with joist-hanger nails. Toenail the front rafter ends to the beam with 8d nails at layout lines. OPTION: You may use rafter ties to attach the rafters to the beams (step 9, page 108).

Purlins

Planned
wall location

9 "Purlins" are spacers that fit between the rafters, flush with the tops, to create a nailing surface for the strips used to mount most panel roof systems. Cut purlins from the same dimension lumber as the rafters, and nail them between the rafters with 8d nails (endnailing through the rafters where possible, toenailing in tighter spots). Use the layout lines drawn on the rafters in step 7 as an installation guide. NOTE: In our plan, we used 2 × 4s for purlins that fit over the planned wall locations, to allow clearance for the top plate that fits between the outer rafters (step 5, page 120).

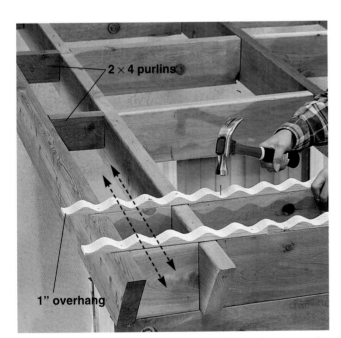

2 × 4 purlins

1" overhang

10 Attach closure strips (page 114) to the tops of the purlins with 6d finish nails. The strips should overhang the outer rafters by 1". Proper alignment of the roof panels depends on the alignment of the closure strips, so make sure the peaks are all aligned before fastening the strips.

11 Measure from the back of the ledger cutout to the ends of the rafters, add 1" for a roof overhang, and cut roof panels to that length using a circular saw with a panel-cutting blade. For easier cutting, gang panels together, sandwiching them between two boards.

(continued next page)

Overlap (rafter location)

12 Begin installing the roof panels. Panels are manufactured so the seams will line up over rafters that are spaced 24" on center. You may need to rip-cut the first panel to span two rafters that are less than 24" apart, as in the photo above. Make sure the panels fit snugly over the closure strips mounted to the purlins. Attach the panels through the peaks, not the troughs, at each purlin location, by driving a 1½" hex-head panel screw with a rubber gasket at every fourth or fifth peak. Predrill through the panel at each screw location, using a bit that is slightly larger than the diameter of the screw shank. Apply caulk in the trough nearest the panel seam before attaching the next panel (see step 14).

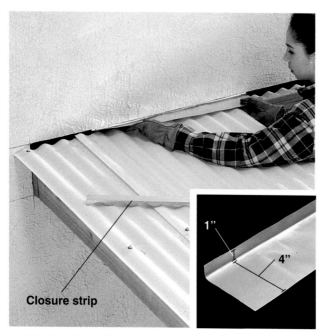

Closure strip

1"
4"

13 After installing one or two panels, begin installing flashing between the roof and the wall. Cut strips of 5"-wide galvanized roll flashing and bend them to create a 1" flange, using a 2 × 4 as a bending jig (inset). Tuck the 1"-wide flange behind the wall covering, then apply caulk to the flat face of a piece of closure strip and insert it between the panels and the underside of the flashing.

14 Continue installing roof panels and flashing, making sure that the panel seams line up over rafters and that the strips of flashing overlap by 3" to 4". Remember to apply caulk to the last trough of each panel so it creates a waterproof seam with the first peak of the next panel.

Techniques for
Building Patio Enclosures

How to Install Walls, Windows & Doors

Build standard 2 × 4 stud walls for patio enclosures, creating rough openings sized for the windows and doors. Follow the door and window manufacturer's installation instructions.

Everything You Need:

Tools: basic hand tools, speed square, reciprocating saw.

Materials: framing lumber, washers and nuts for J-bolts, nails, self-tapping masonry screws (for stucco), drip-edge flashing, stop molding, combination storm windows, storm door, 1 × 4 cedar.

1 Cut 2 × 4 sole plates from pressure-treated lumber, sized to fit against the posts and house wall on all three exposed sides of the patio. Set the sole plates next to the J-bolts installed in the footing (page 114), and mark the locations of the J-bolts onto the plates with a square. Drill centered guide holes into the sole plates at the J-bolt locations.

2 Set the guide holes over the footings so the guide holes slip over the J-bolts. Secure the sole plates by attaching washers and nuts to the J-bolts.

3 Mark locations for the wall framing members onto the sole plates, using your construction plan as a guide. Mark the opening for the door onto the sole plate—usually ⅜" wider than the width of the door.

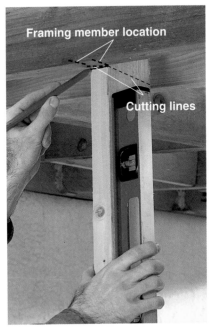

4 Cut 2 × 4s for full-height framing members so they are 2" longer than their finished height. Set them in position onto the sole plates, and use a level to adjust each 2 × 4 until it is plumb. Mark cutting lines on the 2 × 4 where it meets the bottom of the outer rafter. Also mark the position of the 2 × 4 onto the rafters. Cut at cutting lines.

(continued next page)

5 Cut and install the top plates. For this project, we installed 2 × 6 plates between the outer rafters and beams—5½"-wide spaces based on the width of the posts. Cut two top plates to span the distance between the ledger and the beam at the front of the patio enclosure. Cut a plate to fit in front, between the two posts. Nail the top plates in place. Here, we nailed through the rafters into the sides of the plates with 10d nails on the sides of the patio enclosure, and we nailed through the beams in front.

6 Toenail full-height framing members to the top plates at the locations marked on the rafter (step 4, page 119) and to the sole plates at layout marks. Use 10d nails. Check with a level to make sure framing members are plumb.

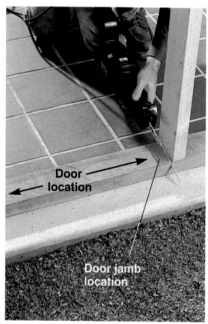

7 Cut and remove the sole plate at the door location, using a reciprocating saw. Make sure you cut next to the framing member marks on your layout—the door jambs should rest on the floor, not the sole plate.

8 Install door jambs. For this project, we used 2 × 6 lumber for the jambs, creating a frame for the door that is centered on the 2 × 4 framing members. Because our door is located next to the house, we attached the inside jamb directly to the siding, using self-tapping masonry screws.

9 Install the door header on top of the door jambs. Our jambs were cut to the rough opening height for the door, so we simply endnailed the 2 × 6 header into the tops of the jambs with 10d nails.

10 Install 2 ×4 headers for the window rough openings, according to your construction plan (window headers usually are installed at the same height as door headers). To set the height for the win- dow headers, attach one end of a chalk line to the top of the door header, slip a line level onto the chalk line, set the line at a level position, and snap it across the other framing members.

Measure down from window-header mark

Finished window-sill location

Rough sill height

11 Measure down from the window header marks to mark positions for the rough windowsills onto the framing members and posts. Remember to in- clude the thickness of the finished windowsill in the rough opening measurement (see step 14 and your construction plan).

12 Cut window headers and rough sills to length from 2 × 4 stock. Install them between framing members by endnailing through the framing mem- bers and into the headers and rough sills where pos- sible. Otherwise, toenail the headers and rough sills in place.

(continued next page)

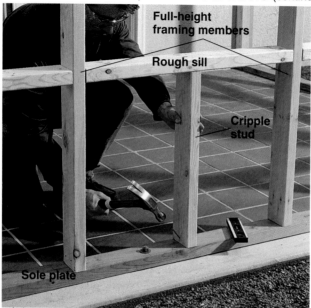

Full-height framing members

Rough sill

Cripple stud

Sole plate

13 Install cripple studs midway between the framing members, fitted between the rough sills and the sole plates, and between the headers and the top plates. Where they meet the top plates, cut the tops of cripple studs to match the angle of the cuts on the full-height framing members.

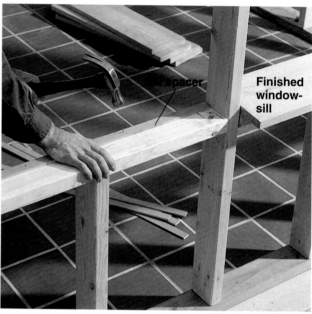

spacer

Finished windowsill

14 Install finished windowsills with a slight slope to direct water runoff away from the structure. To create the slope, tack ¼"-thick sill spacers to the tops of the rough sills, flush with the inside edges. Then, cut the finished sills and attach them to the rough sills with 10d nails so they extend 1" past the edges of the rough sills. Notch out one end of each finished sill to wrap around the outside edge of each framing member.

Window-stop strip

15 Combination storm windows are attached to strips of window-stop molding (we used 1 × 2 pine) mounted at the top and sides of the window opening. Cut strips of 1 × 2 the same length as the headers, then nail them to the bottoms of the headers, flush with the inside edges. Then, cut strips to span from the finished sill to the header strips, and attach them to the jambs with 6d casing nails.

16 Apply a bead of caulk to the outside edges of the 1 × 2 window-stop strips. Set each window in position in the rough opening, pressing it into the caulk beads. Leave a slight gap for drainage between the bottom of the window and the finished sill. NOTE: Combination storm windows usually are not fastened at the bottom.

17 Make sure the window is level and square in the rough opening, then drill pilot holes for #4 × 1" hex-head sheet-metal screws into the flanges of the window. Attach the window starting at the top corners, driving three fasteners into each flange. Install all of the windows.

1 × 4 mullion strip

18 Cover the exposed framing members with 1 × 4 lumber (we used cedar) cut to fit between the window headers and the finished sills. Install the 1 × 4s, called "mullions," so they are centered on the framing members. Use 8d siding nails.

19 Install a combination storm door in the door rough opening, following the manufacturer's directions (see the Black & Decker Home Improvement Library's *Carpentry: Remodeling* for additional storm-door installation information).

Techniques for Building Patio Enclosures

How to Install Wall Coverings & Trim

Installing the wall coverings and trim gives definition and a finished appearance to your patio enclosure project. Choose exterior and interior coverings that match or complement the siding of your house. Use only materials that are rated for outdoor use, like the cedar sheathing we used to clad the project shown here.

Everything You Need:

Tools: basic hand tools, miter box, caulk gun.

Materials: exterior siding, trim boards, siding nails, drip-edge flashing, caulk.

1 To create the exterior walls of our patio enclosure, we used ¼"-thick rough cedar siding panels and 1 × 4 cedar boards to cover the edges and seams (called "battens"). Start with the wall areas below the windows, cutting siding panels to fit the space between the windowsill and the ground—leave a ¼" gap at the bottom. Cut siding panels so the seams fall over framing members, leaving a ⅛" to ¼"-wide expansion gap between panels. Attach panels to framing members with 4d galvanized siding nails.

2 Install trim strips (we used 1 × 4 cedar batten boards) to trim out the seams at the tops and bottoms of the siding panels, and to cover the joints between panels. Arrange the strips so the tops and bottoms run the full length of the wall, if possible, and fill in vertical strips to make butt joints at the tops and bottoms. Use 4d siding nails to attach the batten boards.

3 Before installing siding above the windows and doors, cut strips of drip-edge flashing and attach them to the headers with caulk—do not use fasteners. Drip-edge flashing directs water away from the framing members. TIP: Instead of using prefabricated drip-edge flashing, you can bend metal flashing strips to fit.

124

4 Install siding panels between the headers and the top plates. Cut the siding pieces for the side walls so the top angle matches the slope of the roof line. Attach siding panels, then cut and install battens for the tops and bottoms, and to cover vertical joints. NOTE: You may need to rip-cut the bottom batten to fit around the door header, depending on the construction method used.

5 Caulk all exposed seams, using exterior caulk that is tinted to match the color of the siding.

6 Install 1 × 4 cedar mullions (step 18, page 123) on the inside faces of the vertical framing members, then cut and install siding panels on the interior sides of the walls, using the same techniques used on the exterior. For the interior of our project, we used the same ¼"-thick cedar siding used on the exterior. Instead of 1 × 4 cedar battens, we used pine ranch moldings at the bases of the panels, which were cut to full wall length so there were no seams to cover.

7 Install the remaining interior trim. We used ranch-style baseboards, mitered at the corners. We also installed pine quarter-round molding at the corner joints. If you are using cedar for the trim, no further finishing is required. If you are using pine or exterior-grade plywood, seal or paint the wood for protection and to improve the appearance.

INDEX

Cowles Creative Publishing, Inc.
offers a variety of how-to books.
For information write:
Cowles Creative Publishing
Subscriber Books
5900 Green Oak Drive
Minnetonka, MN 55343